Type ■

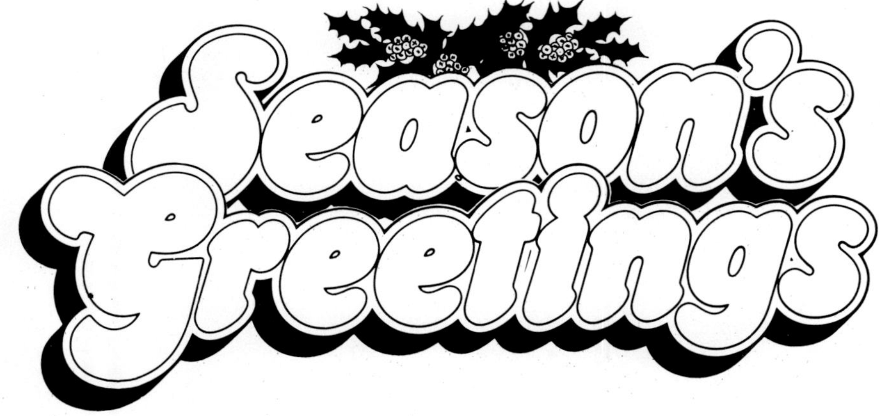

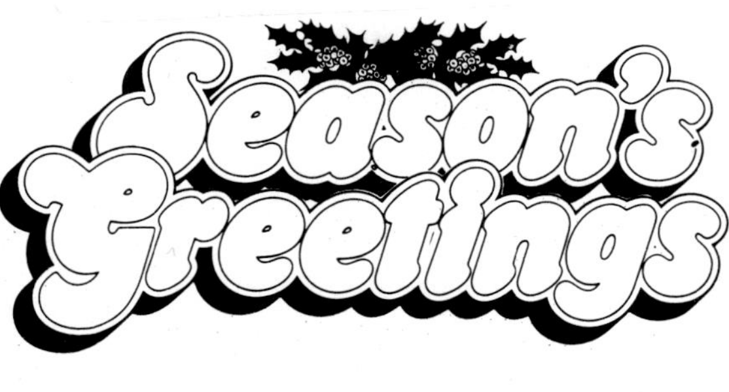

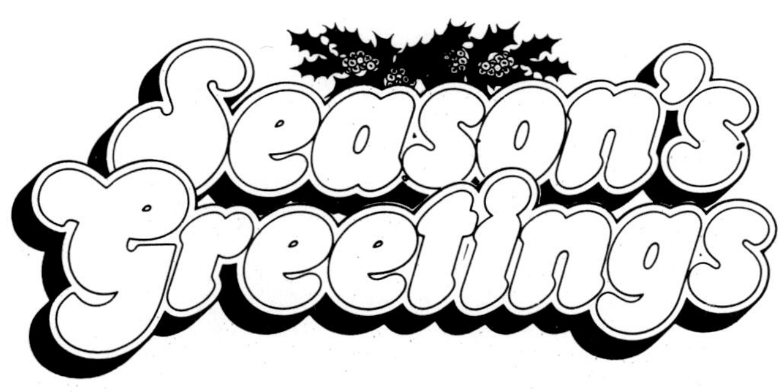

PERFECT PRESENTS

PERFECT PRESENTS

PERFECT PRESENTS

Seasons Greetings

Seasons Greetings

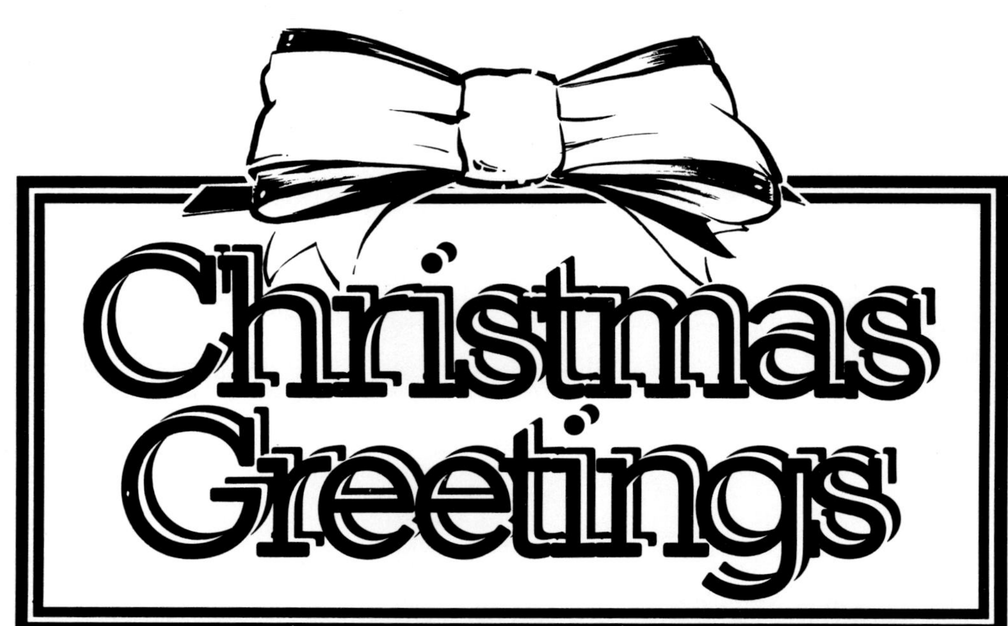

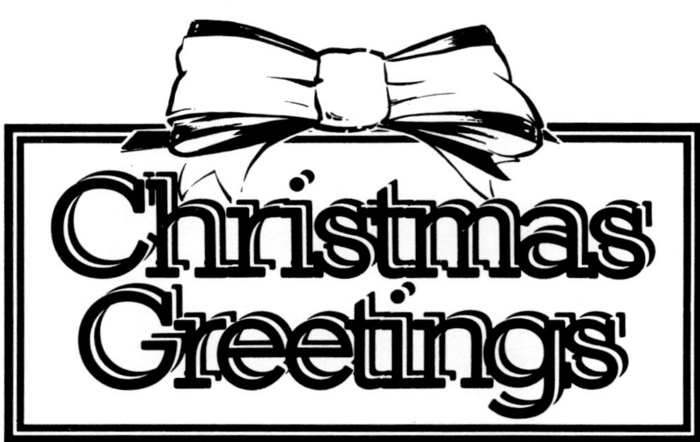

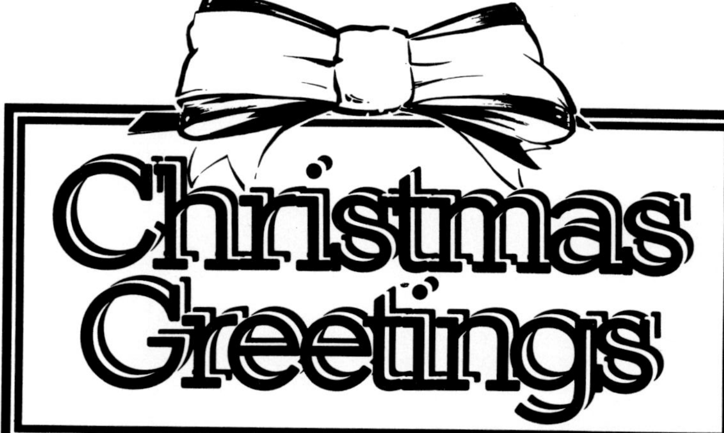

TREES TREES

TREES

Seasons Greetings

Christmas

Christmas

Christmas

Gifts Galore

Gifts Galore

Gifts Galore

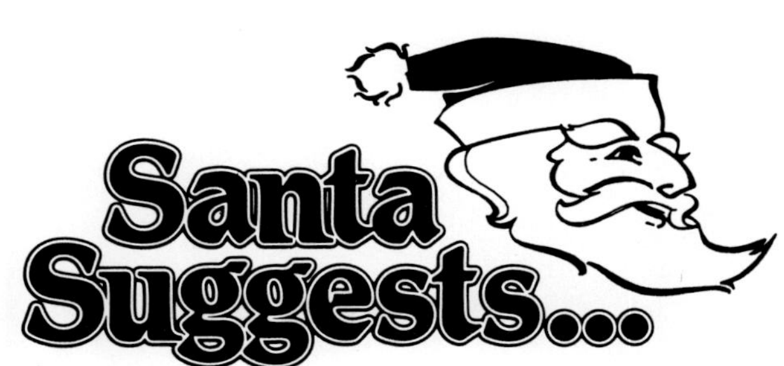

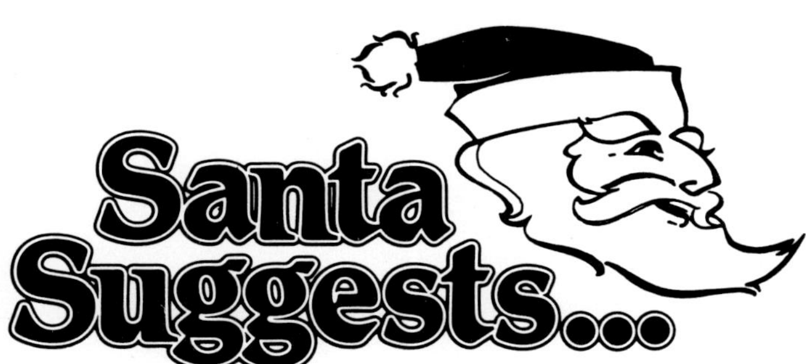

NOEL

NOEL

NOEL

NOEL

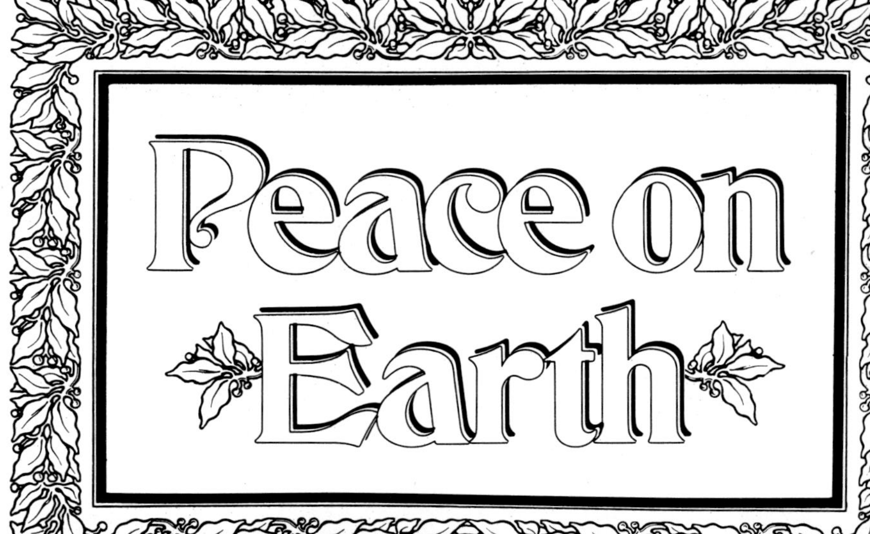

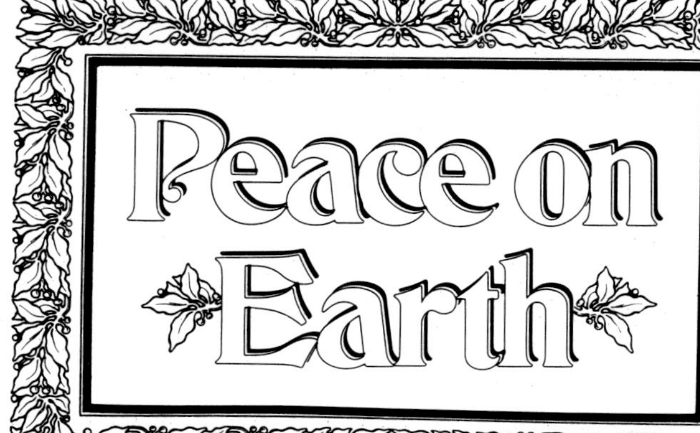

Peace on Earth

Santa Suggests...

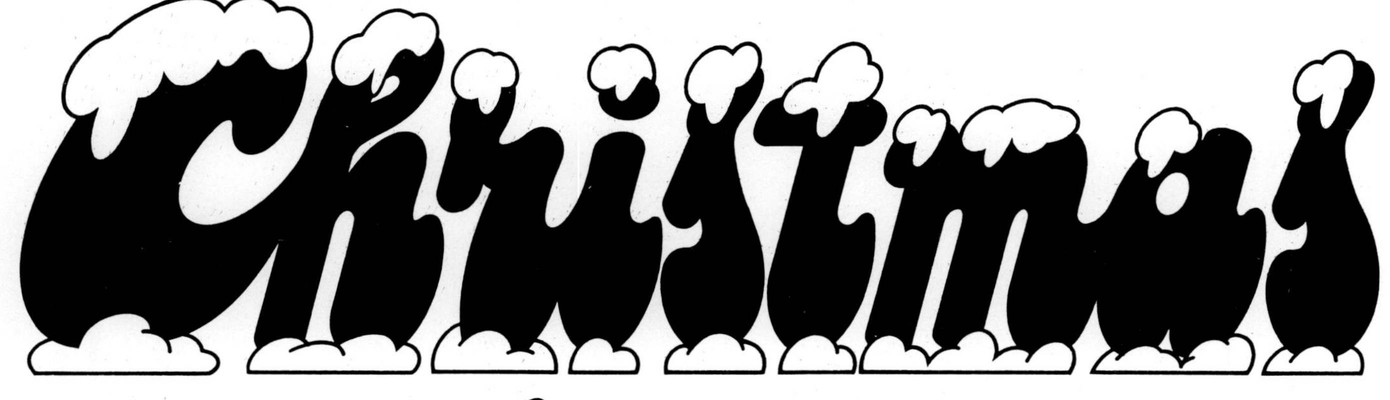

Christmas
Seasons Greetings
Gifts
Seasons Greetings
Gifts
Seasons Greetings
Gifts
Christmas
Christmas

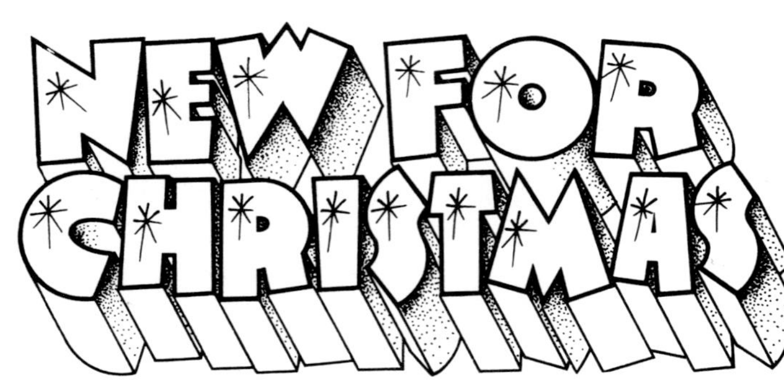

NEW FOR CHRISTMAS

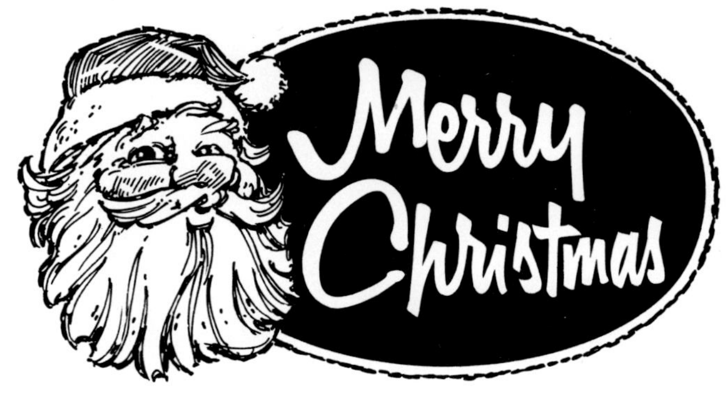

Merry Christmas

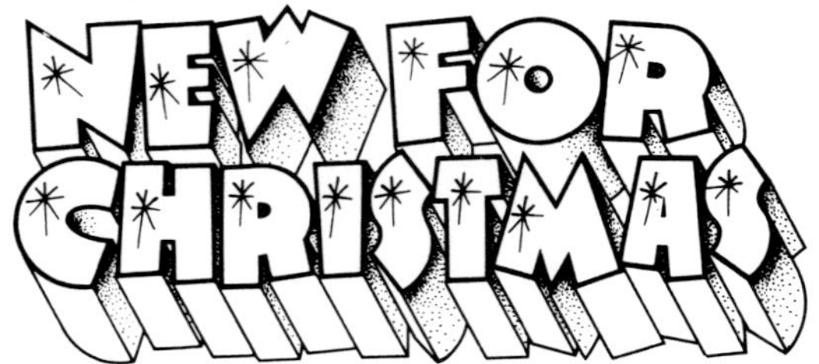

NEW FOR CHRISTMAS

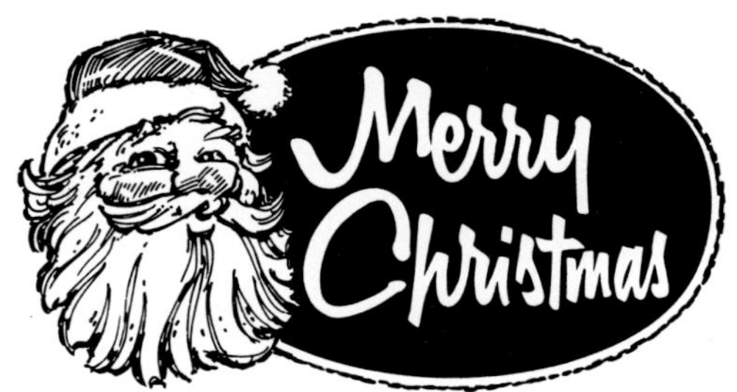

Merry Christmas

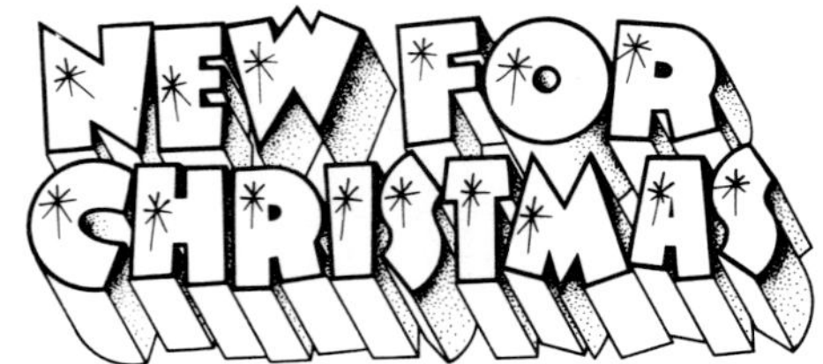

NEW FOR CHRISTMAS

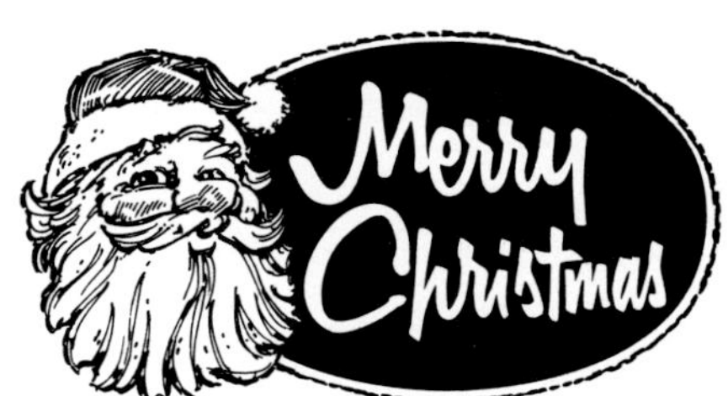

Merry Christmas

Gift Ideas
Gift Ideas
Gift Ideas

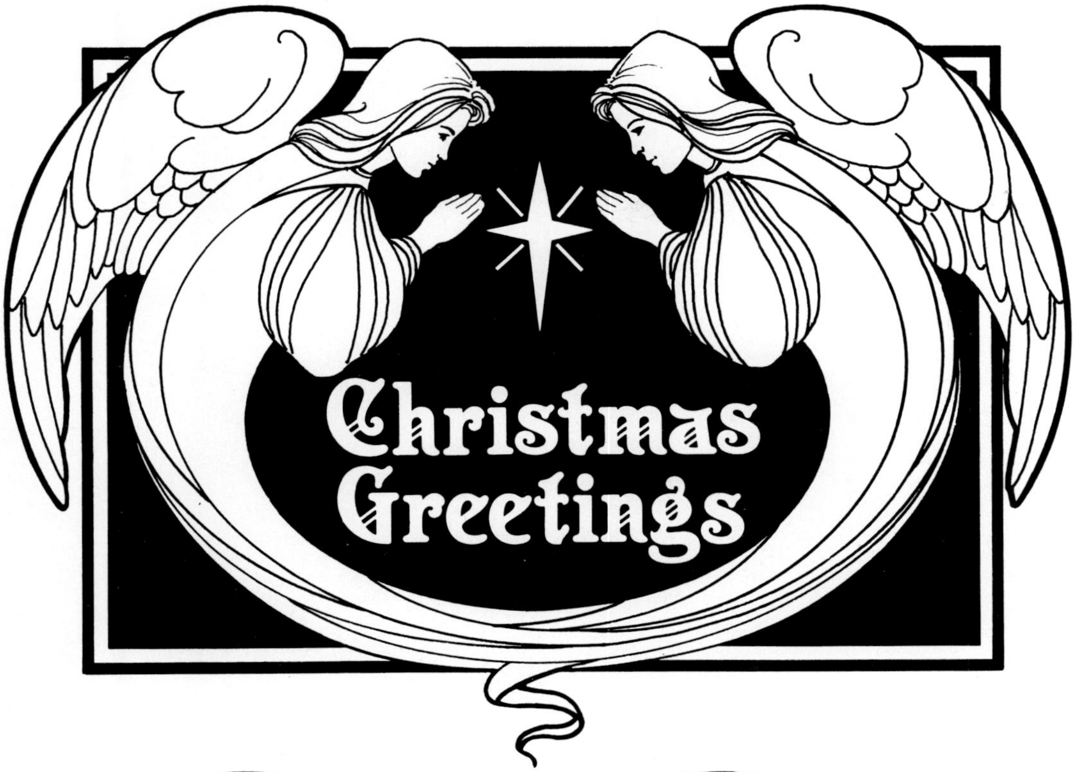

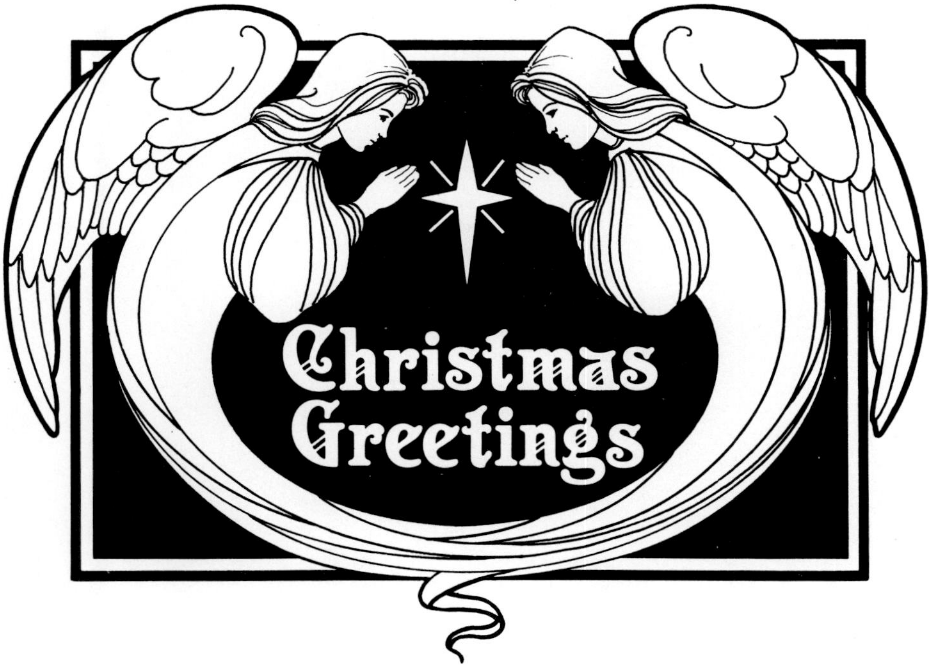

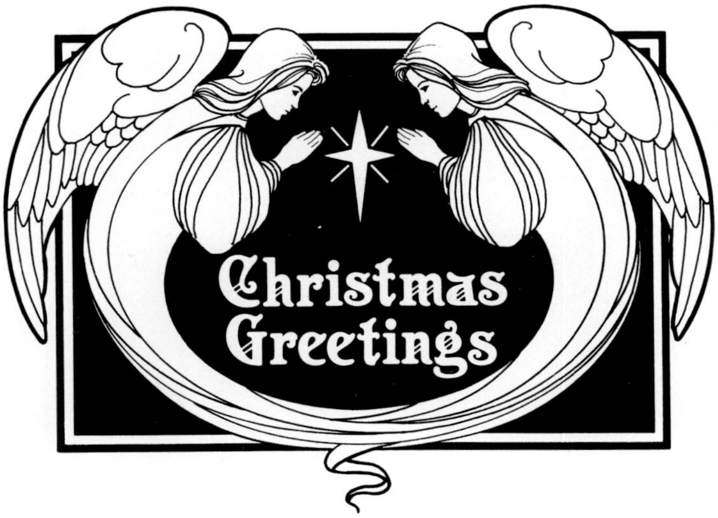

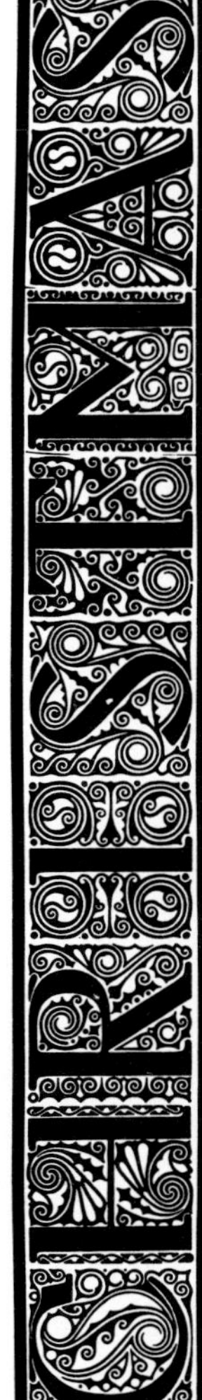

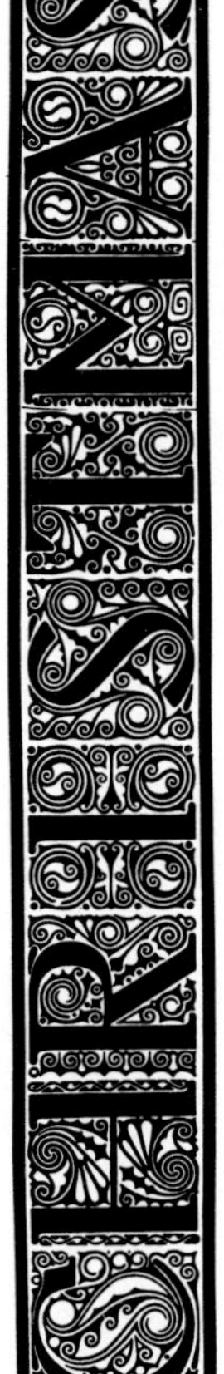

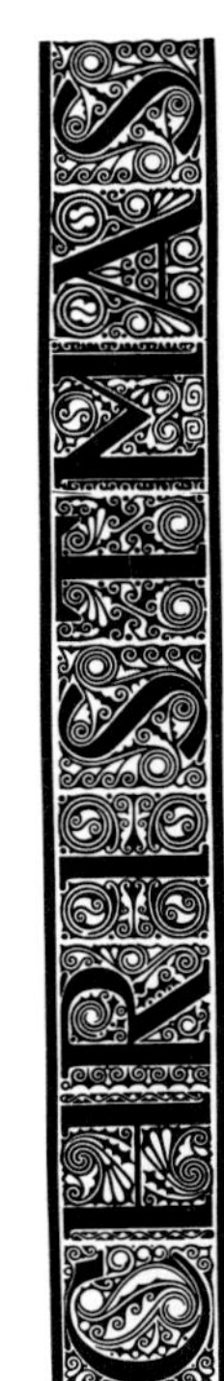

■ Spots

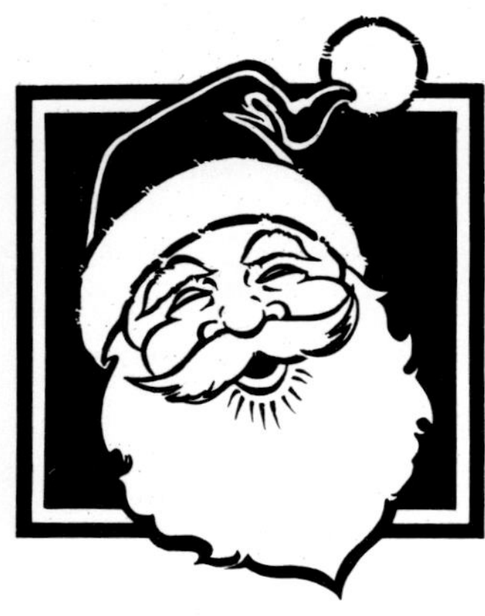 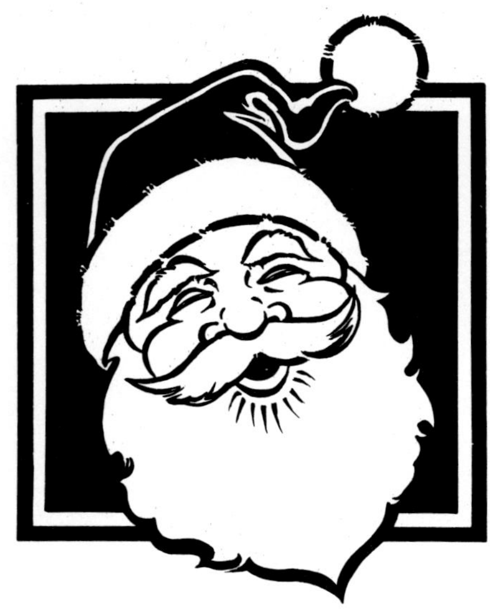 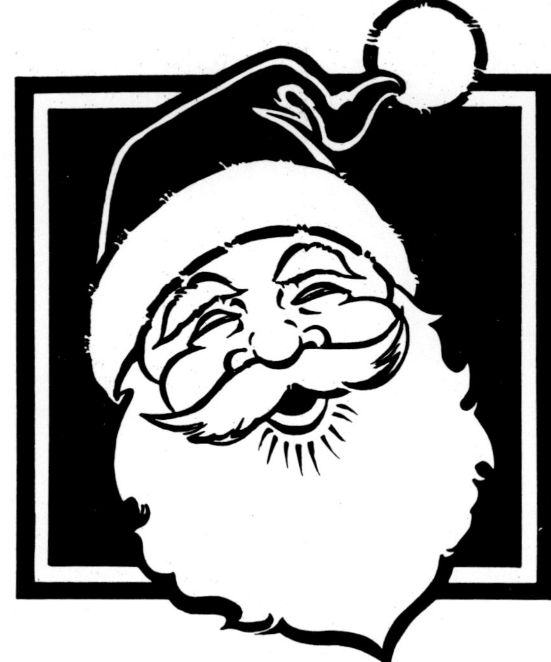

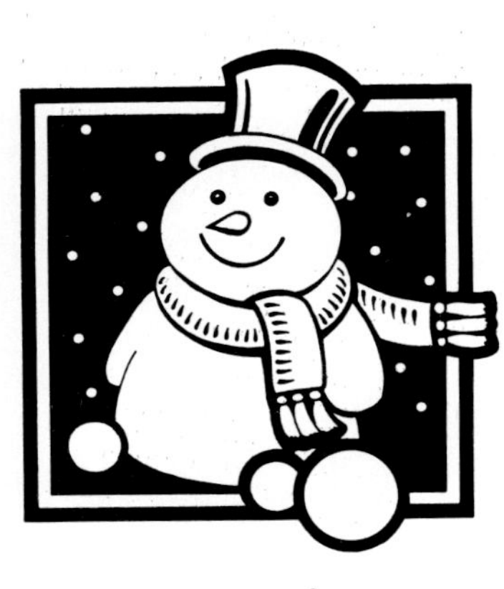 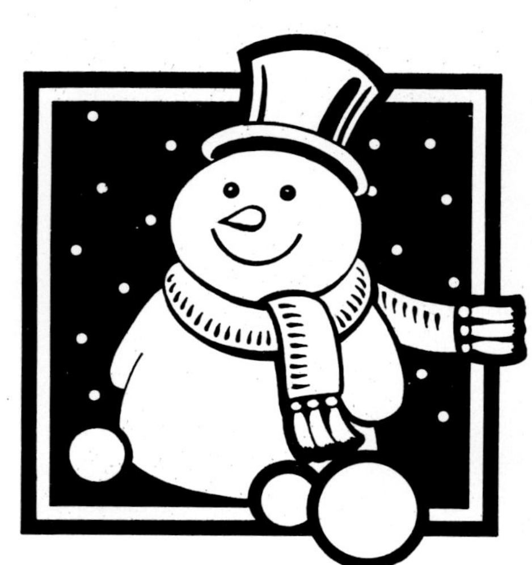 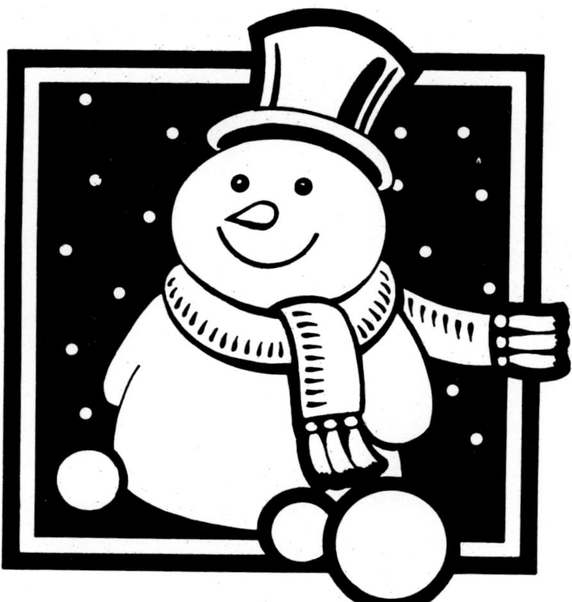

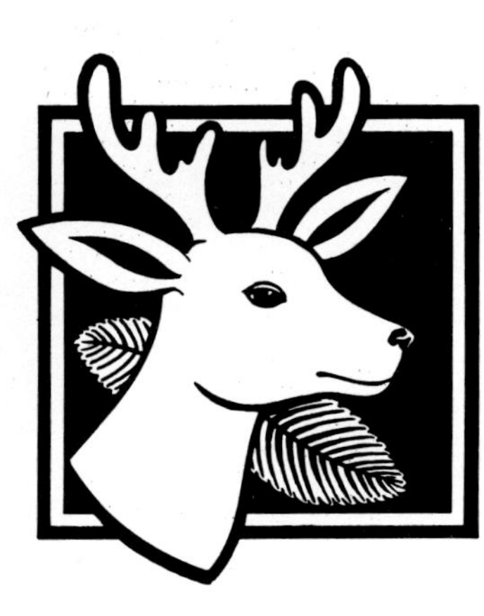 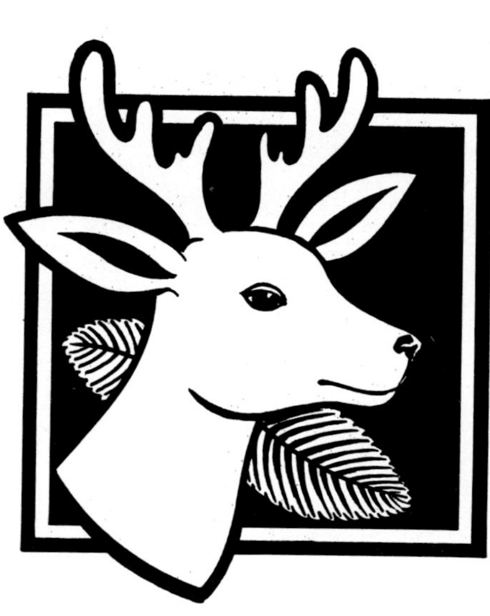 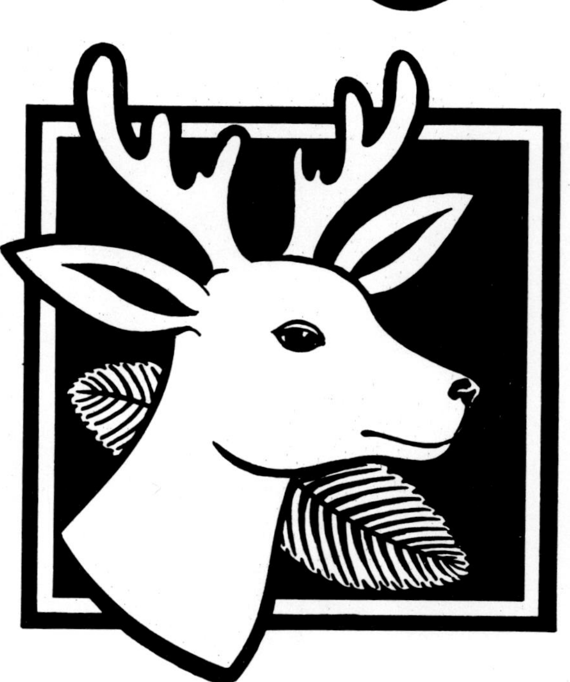

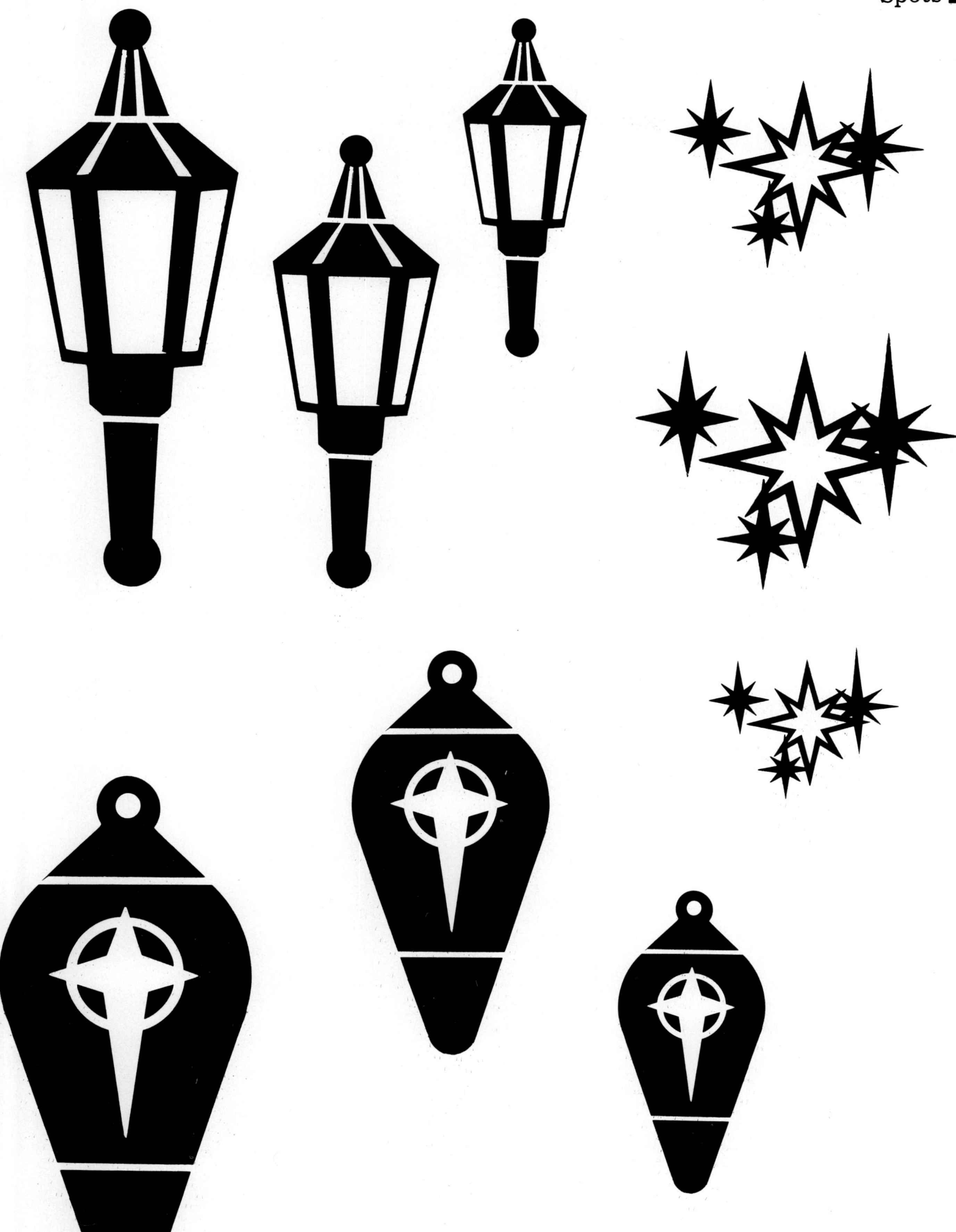

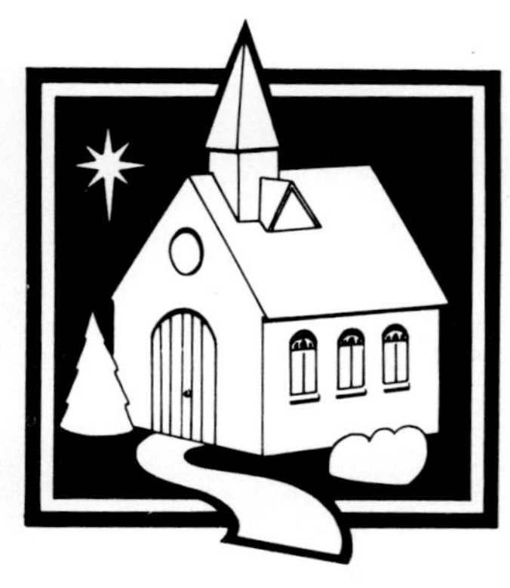
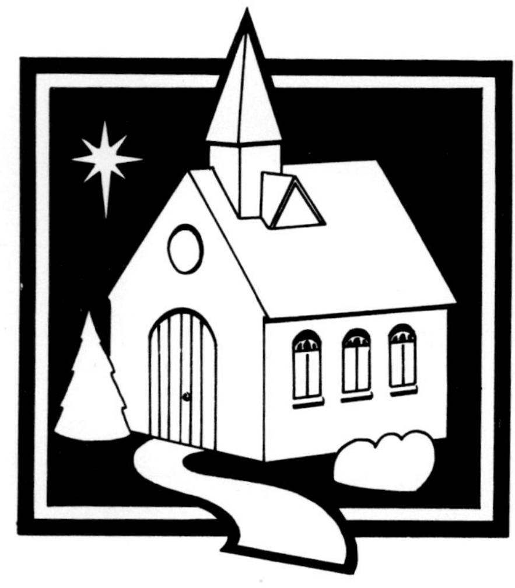
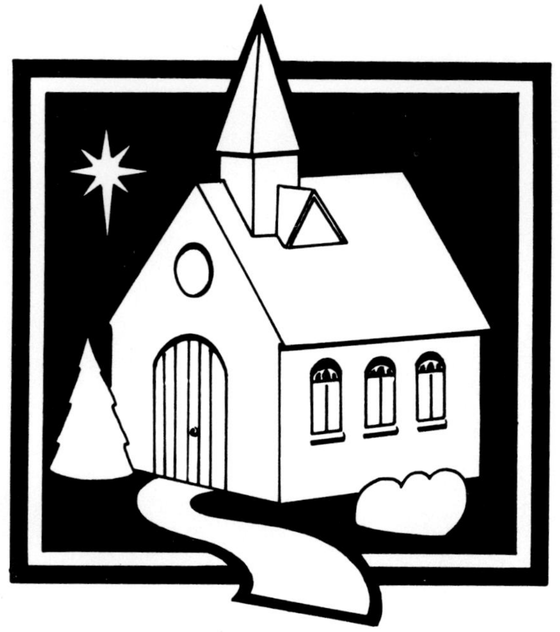
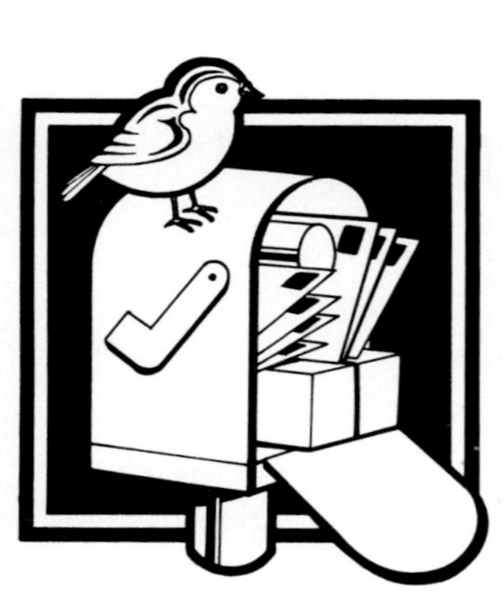
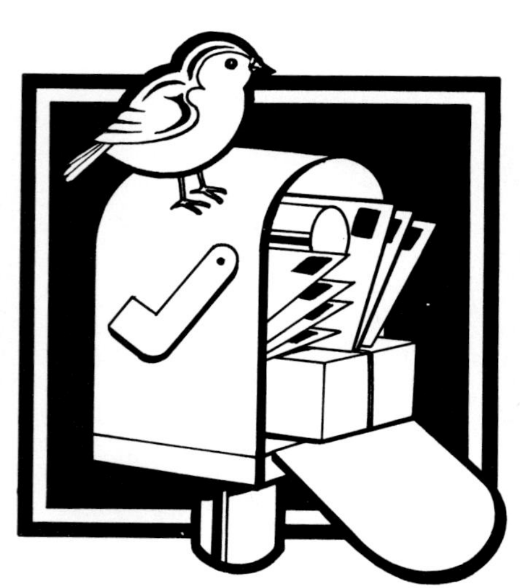
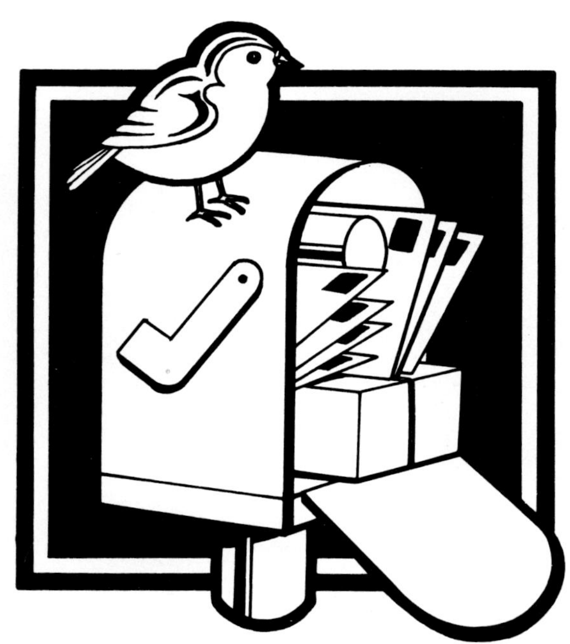
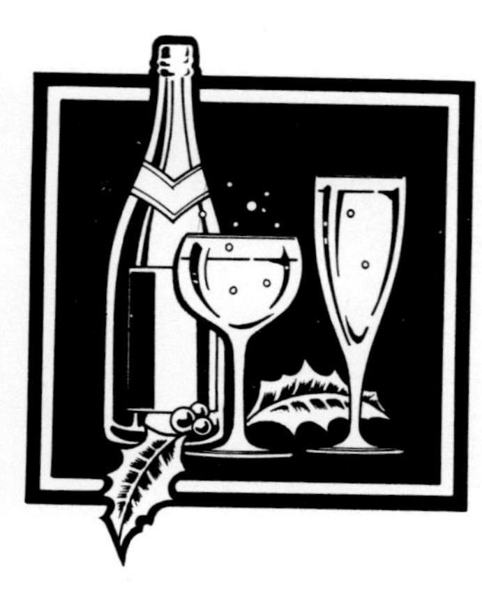
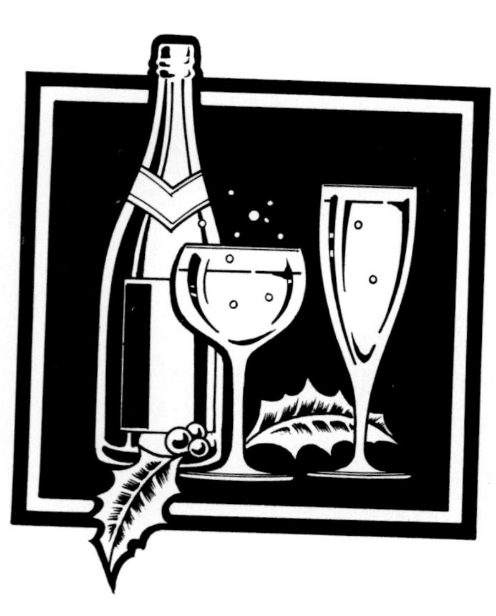
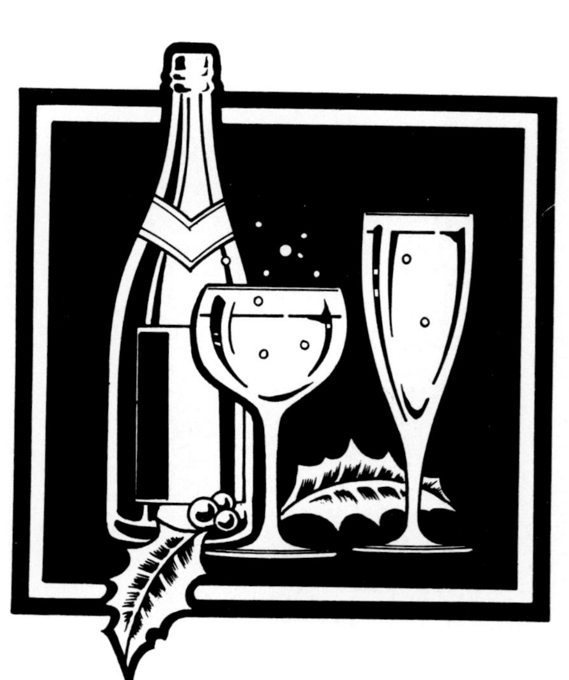

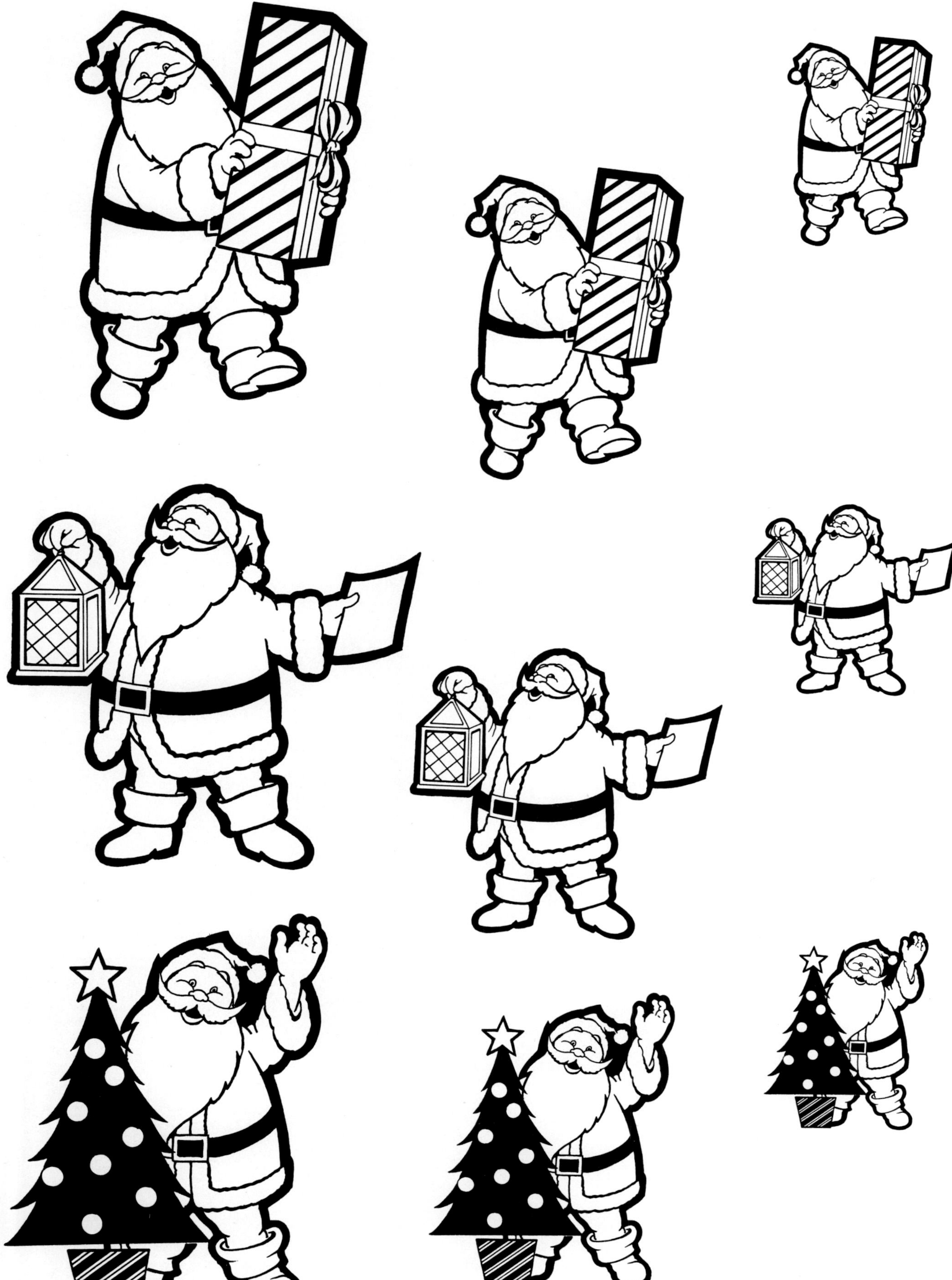

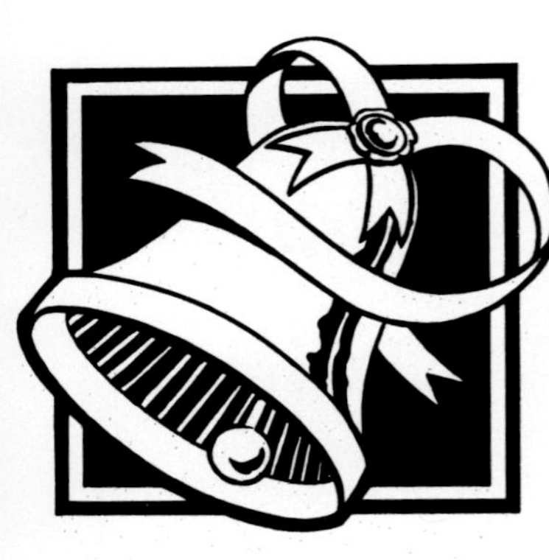
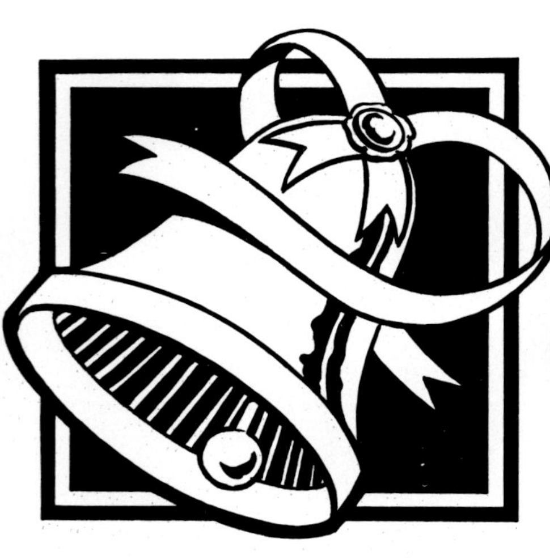
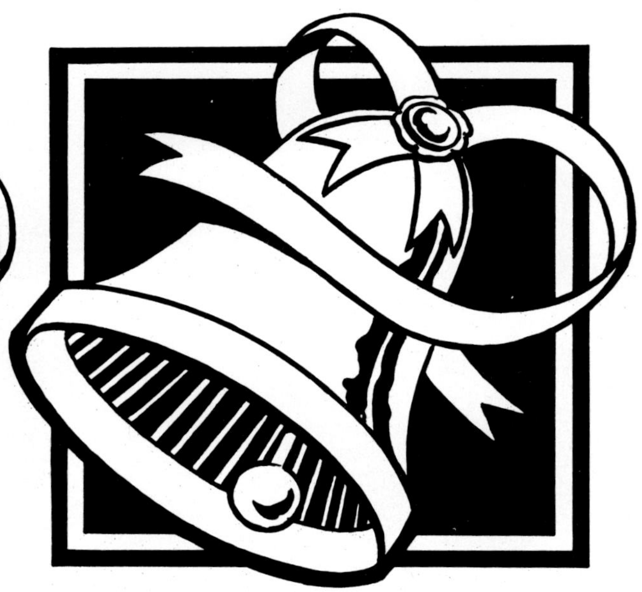
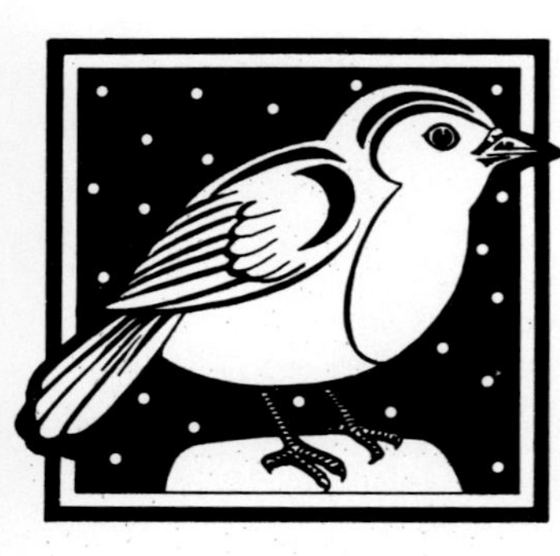
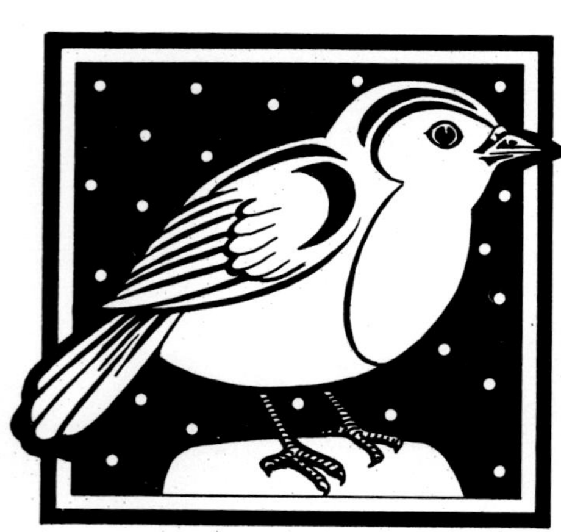
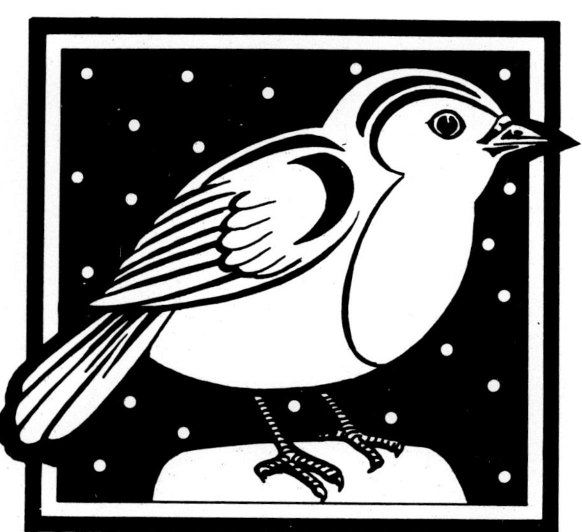
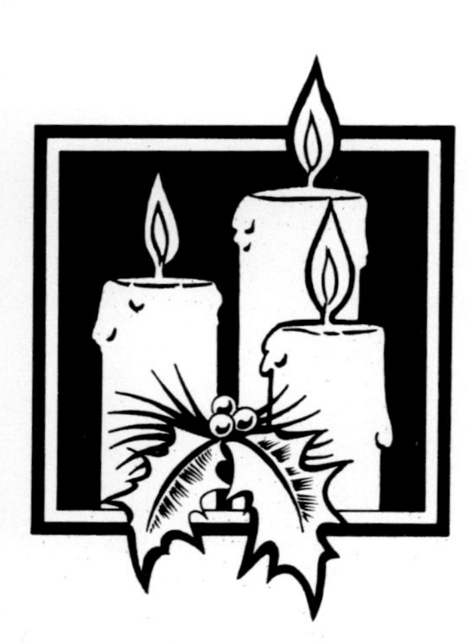

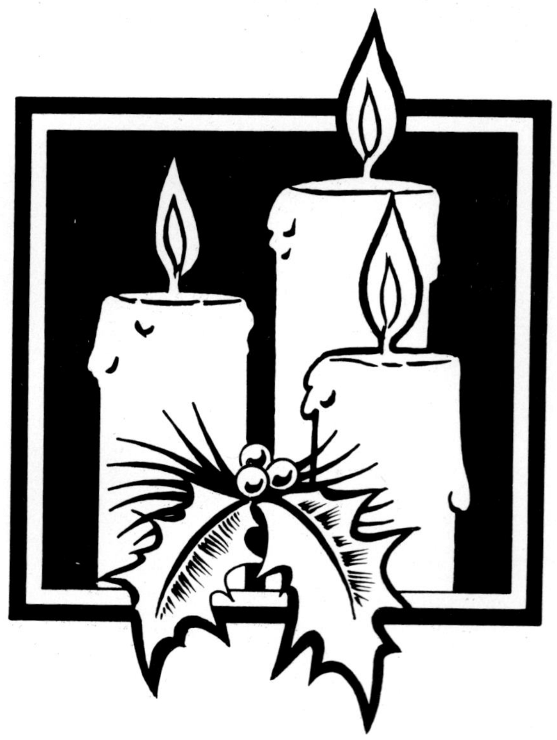

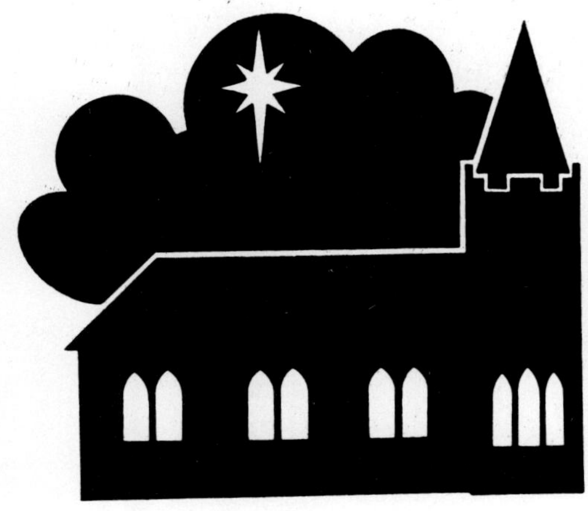
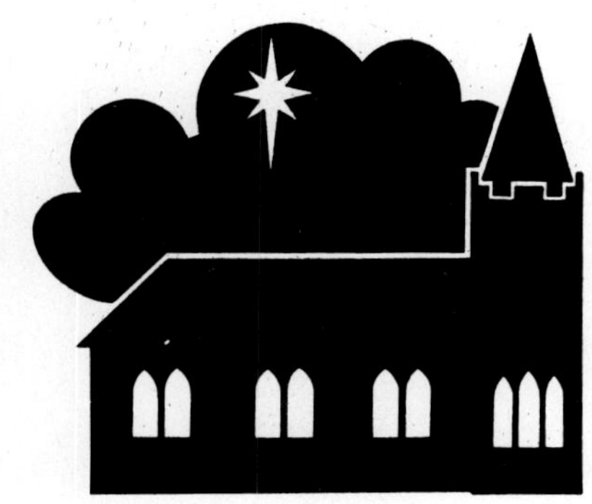
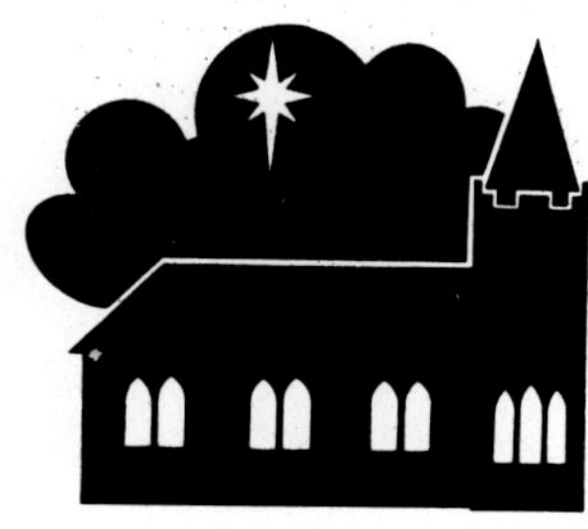
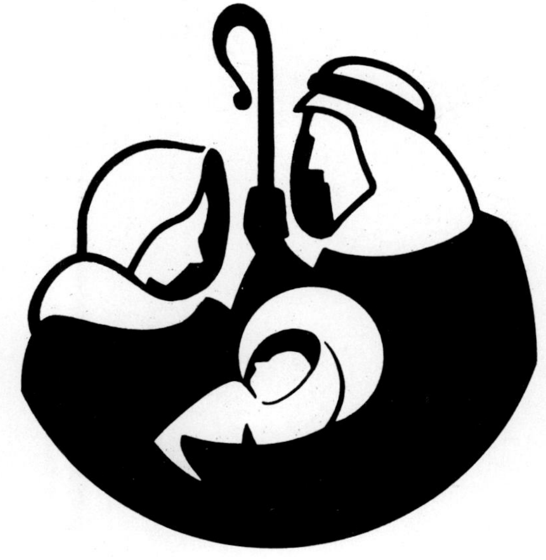
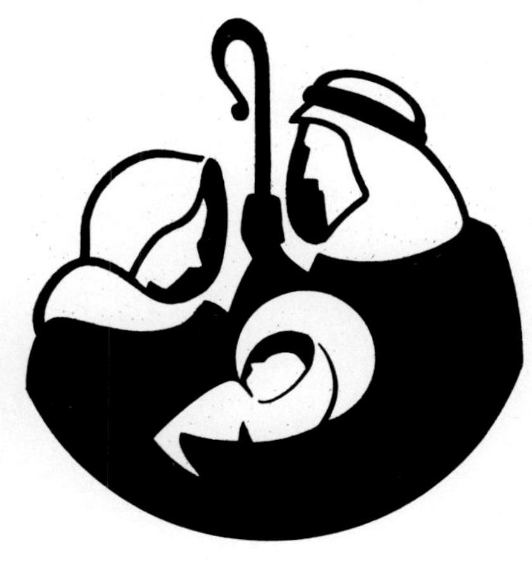
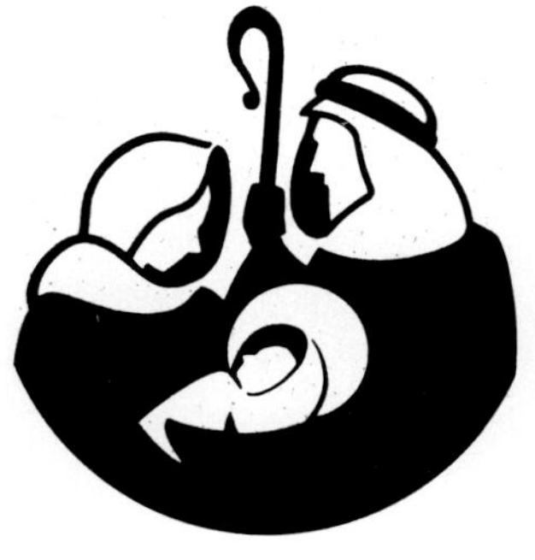
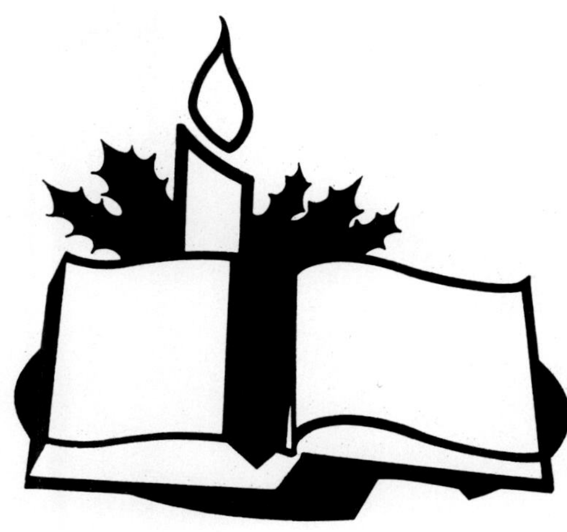
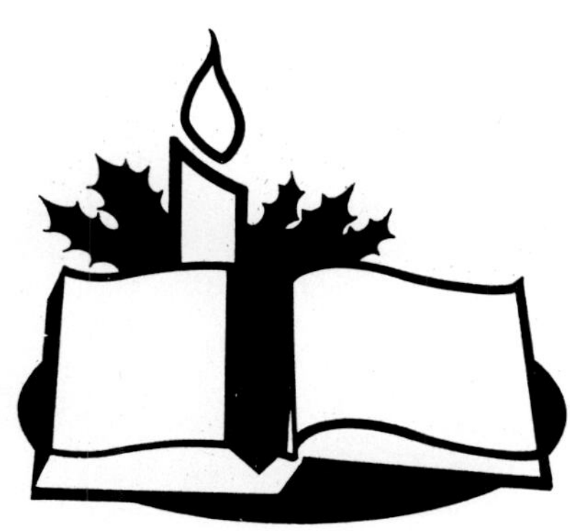

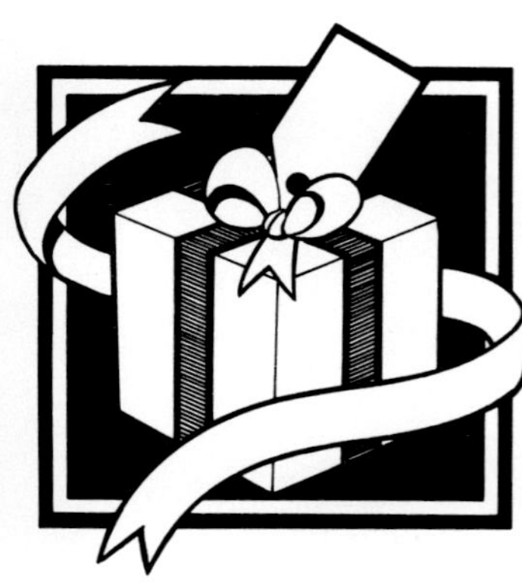
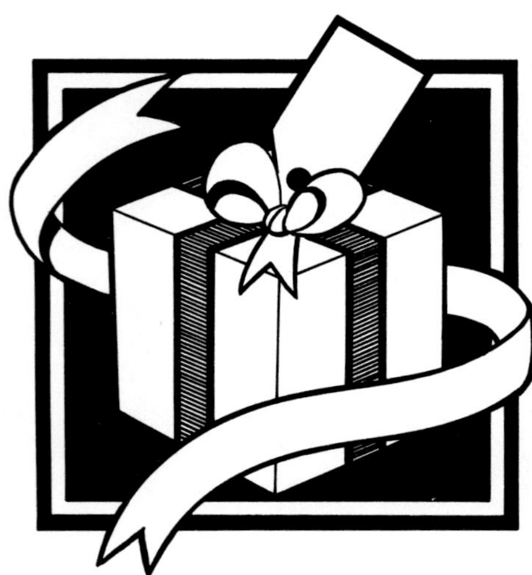
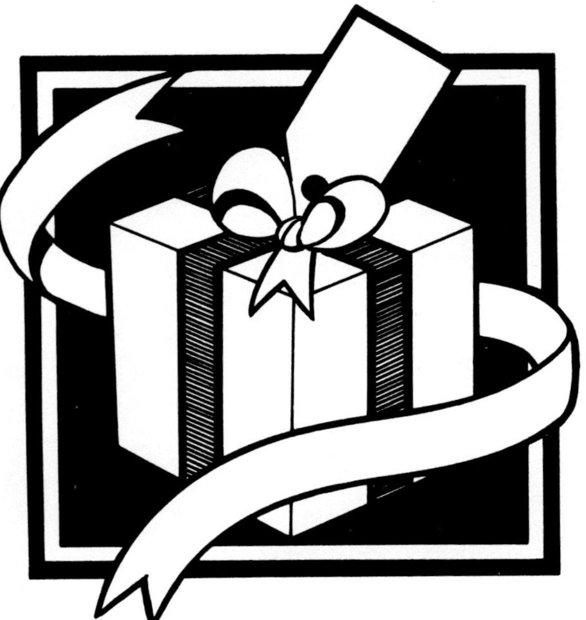
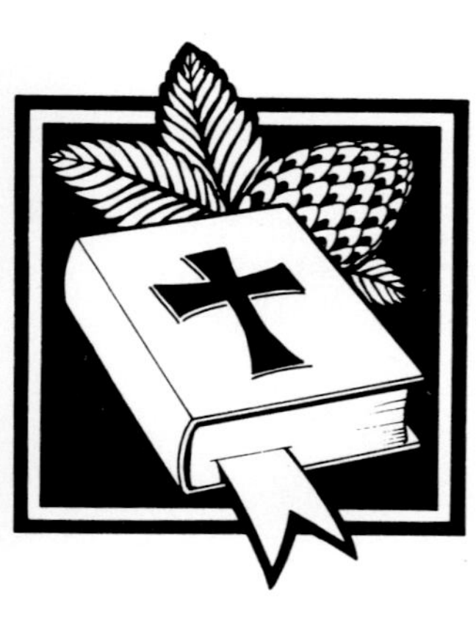
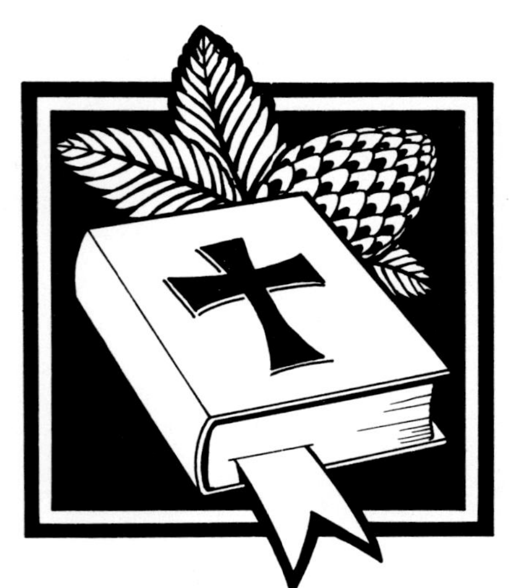
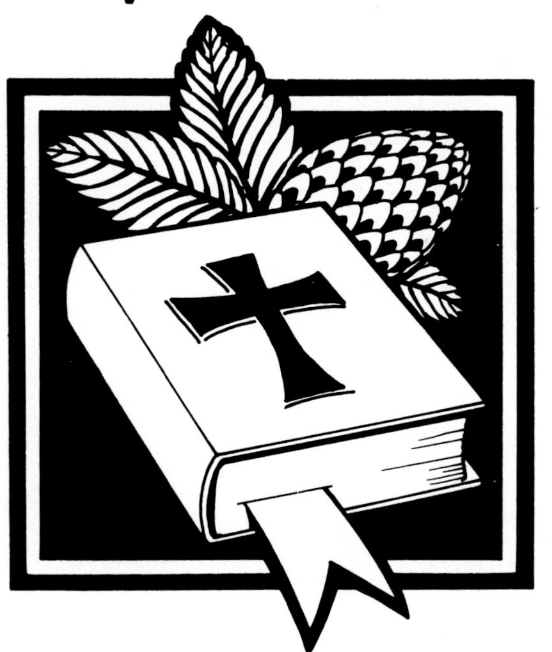
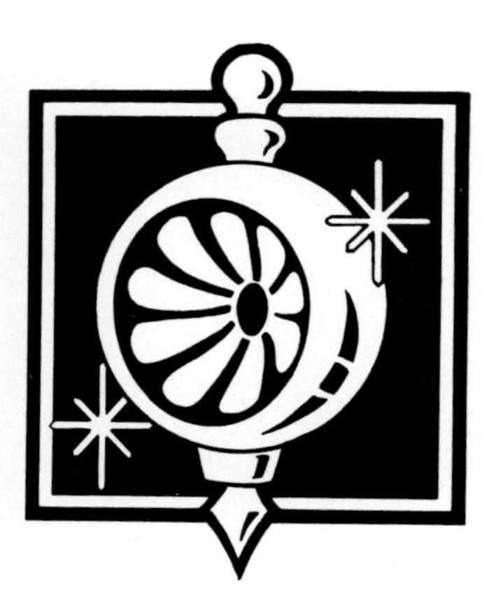
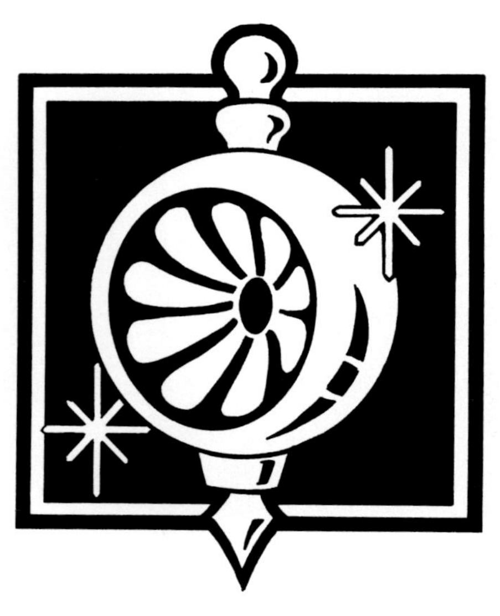
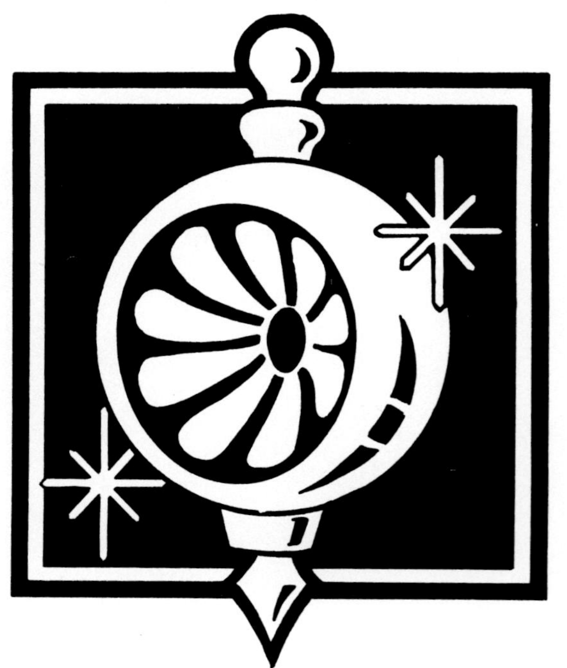

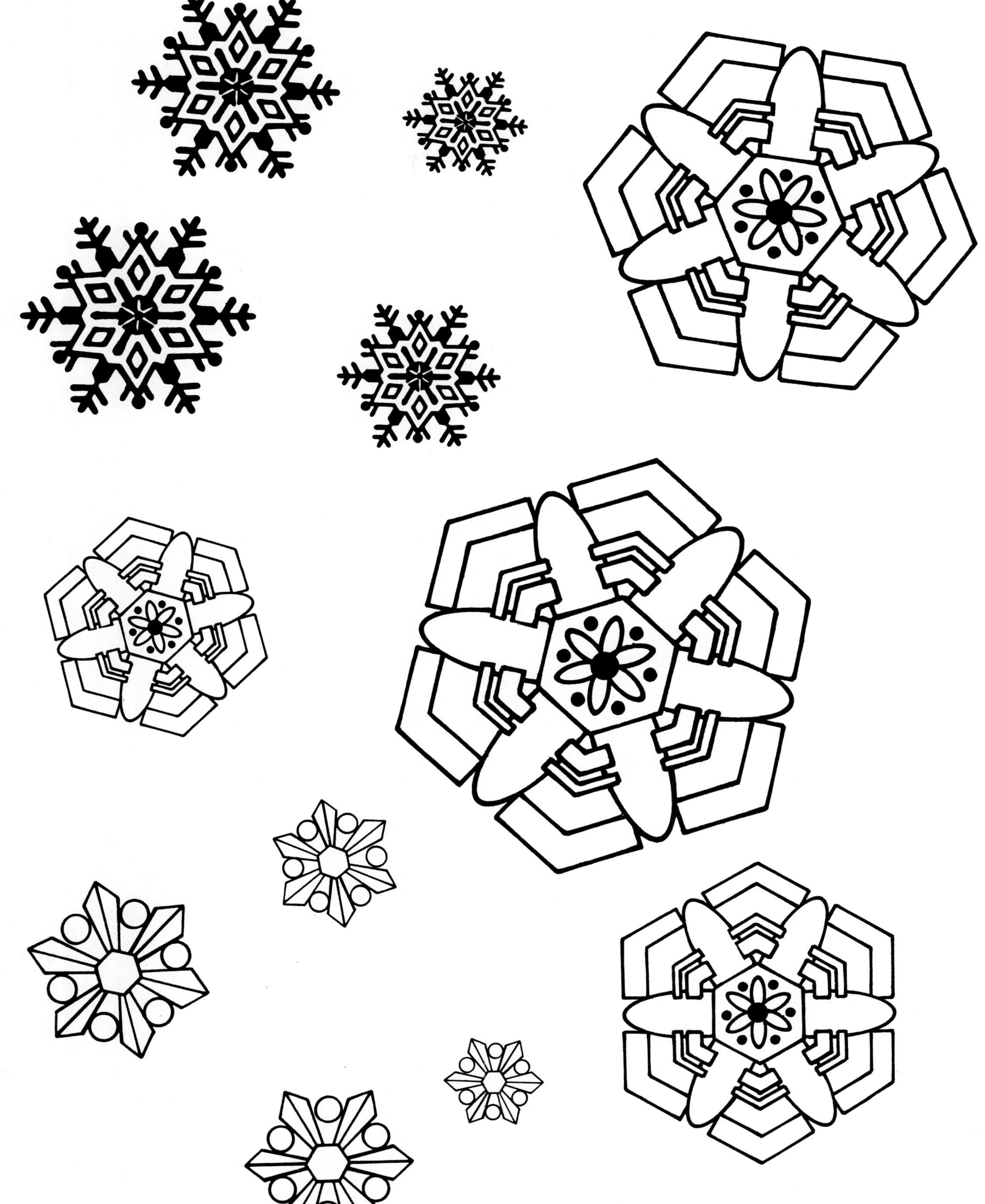

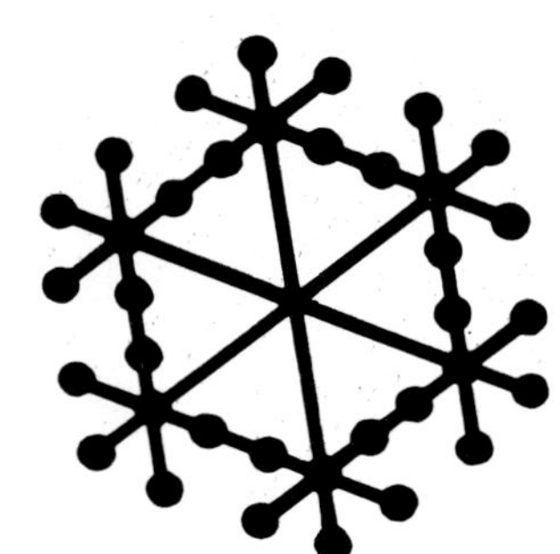
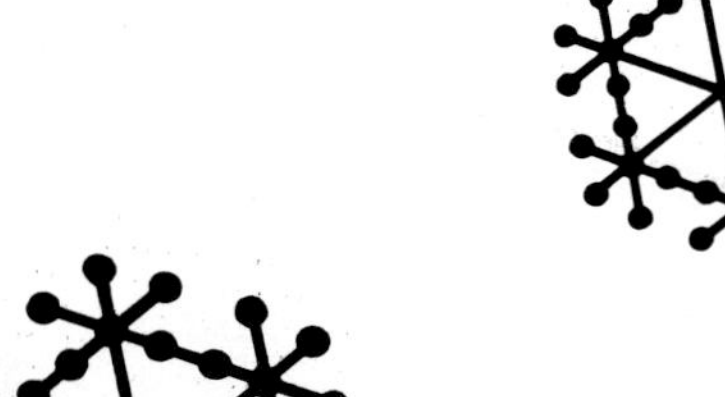
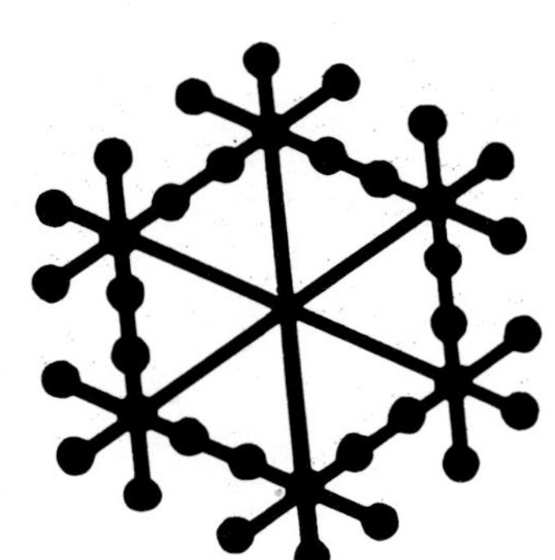
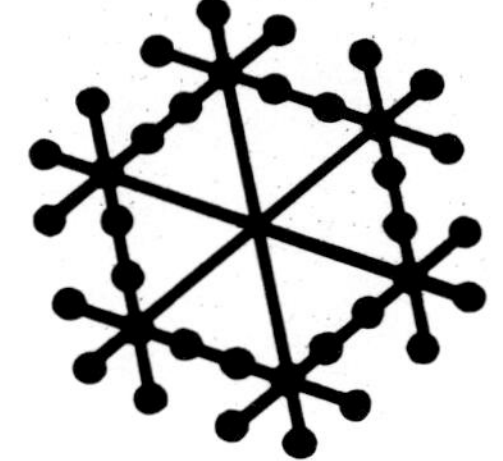
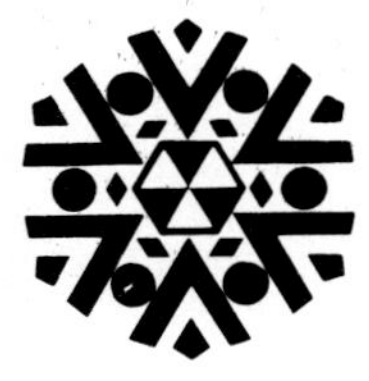
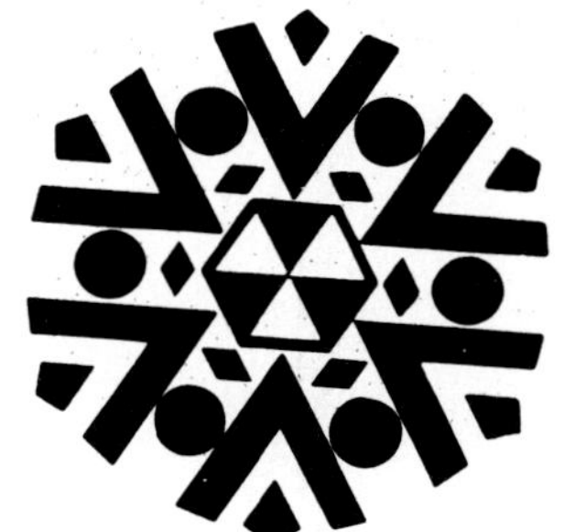
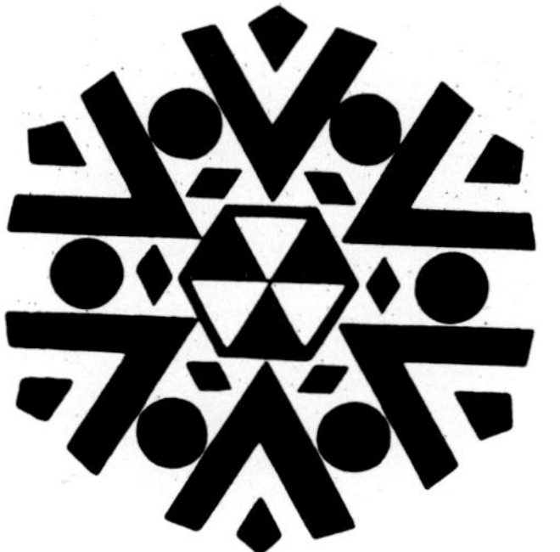
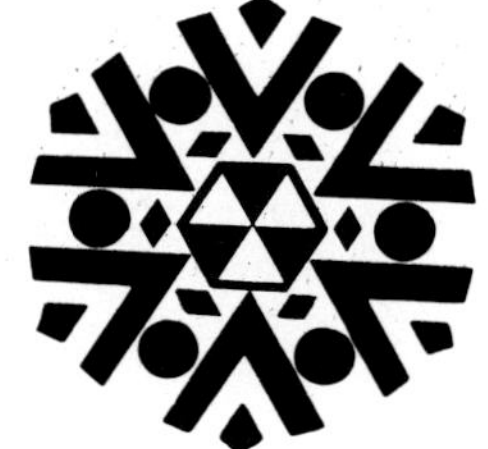
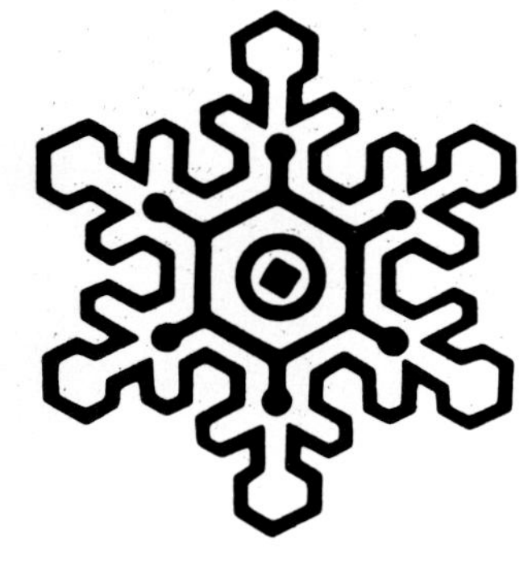

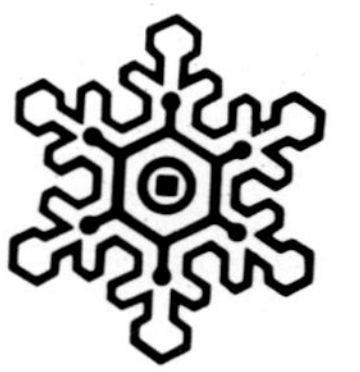
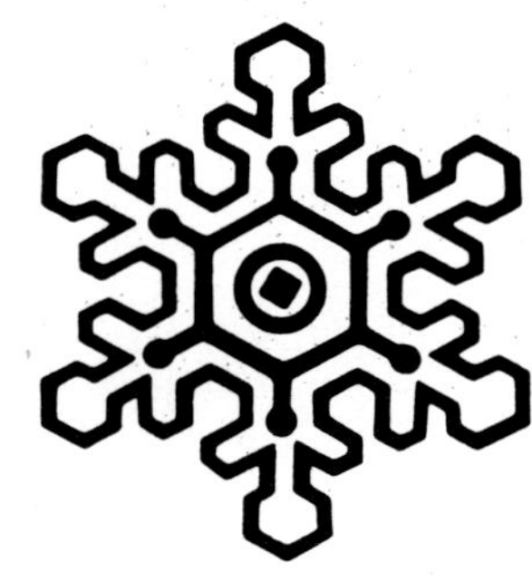

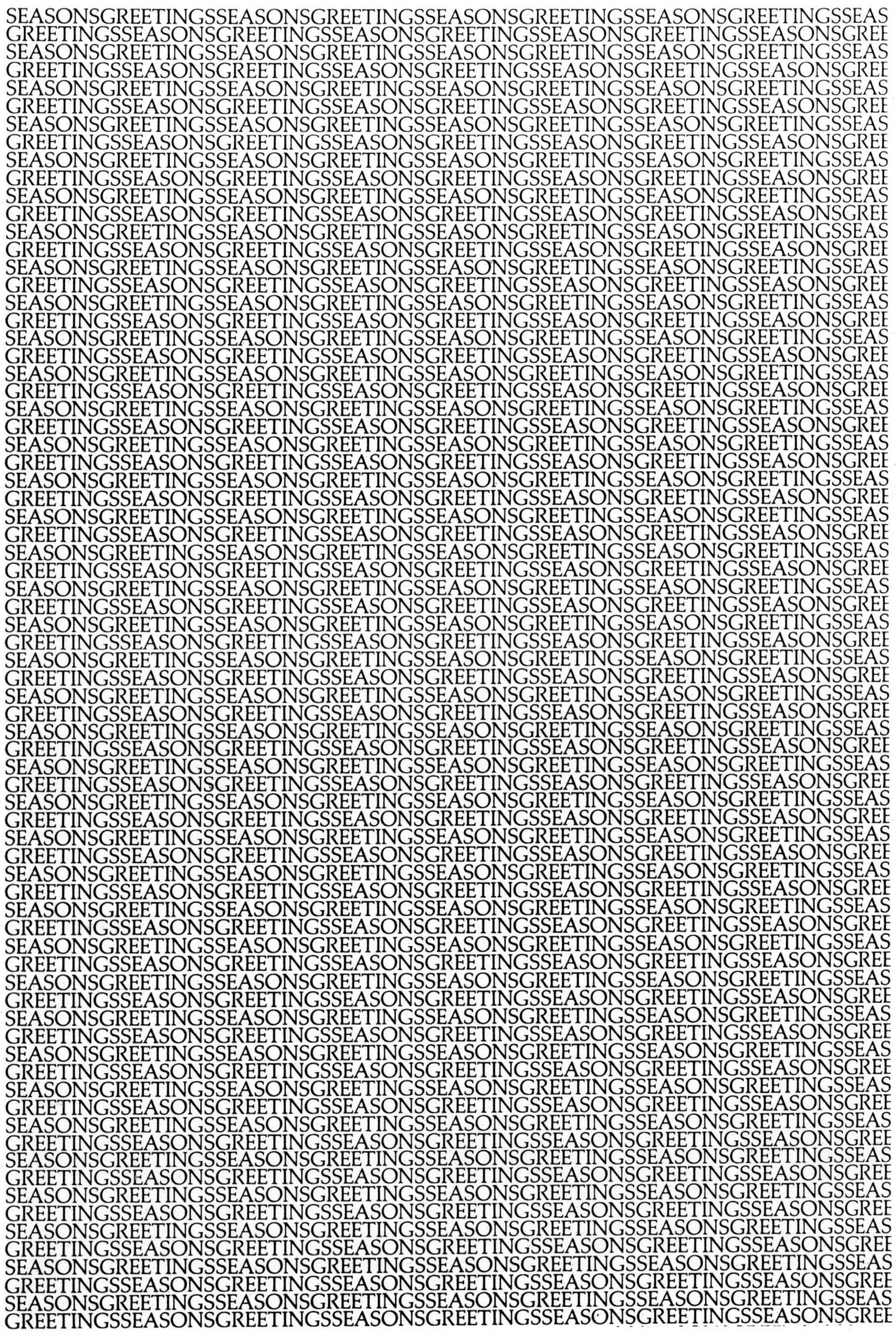

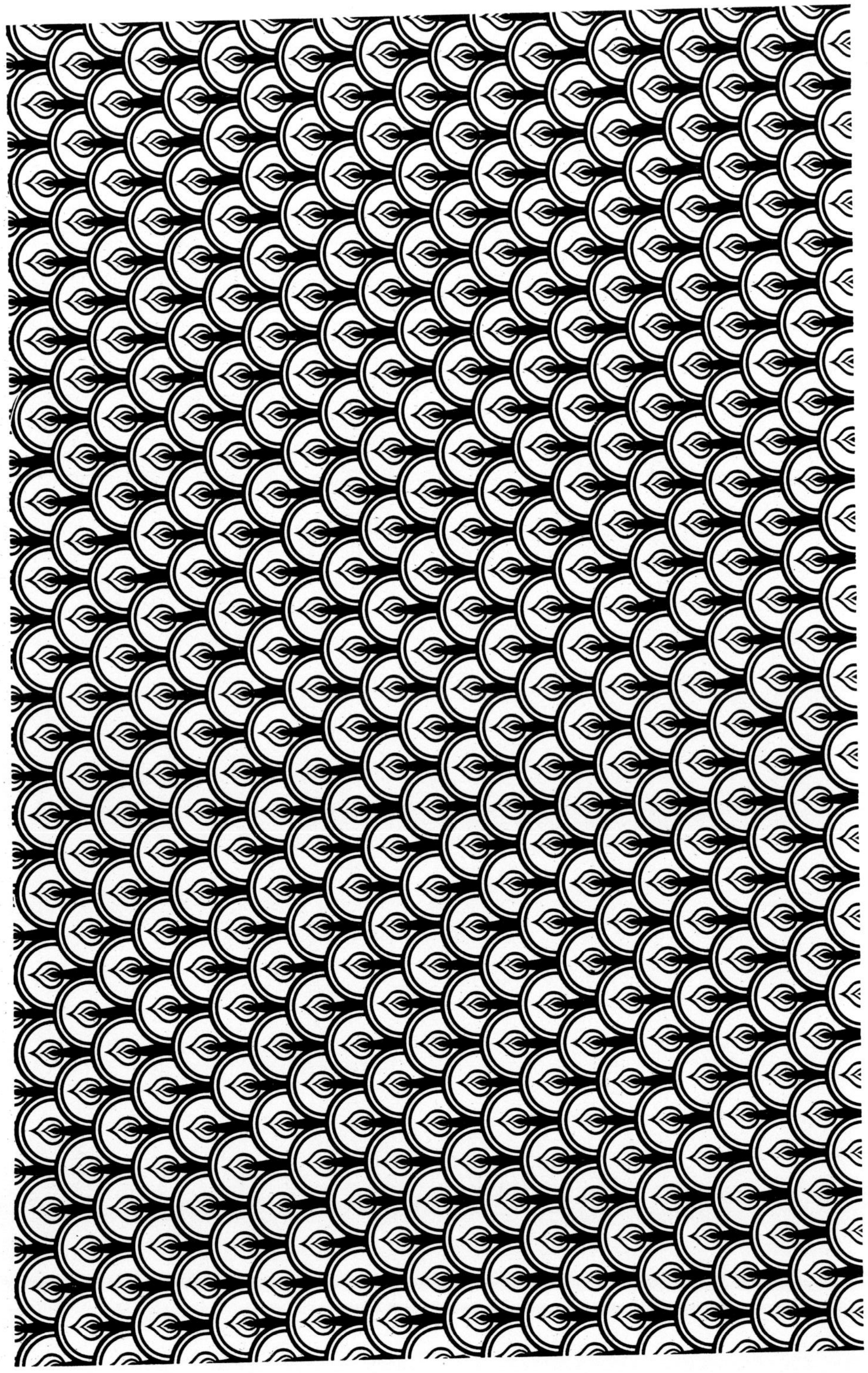

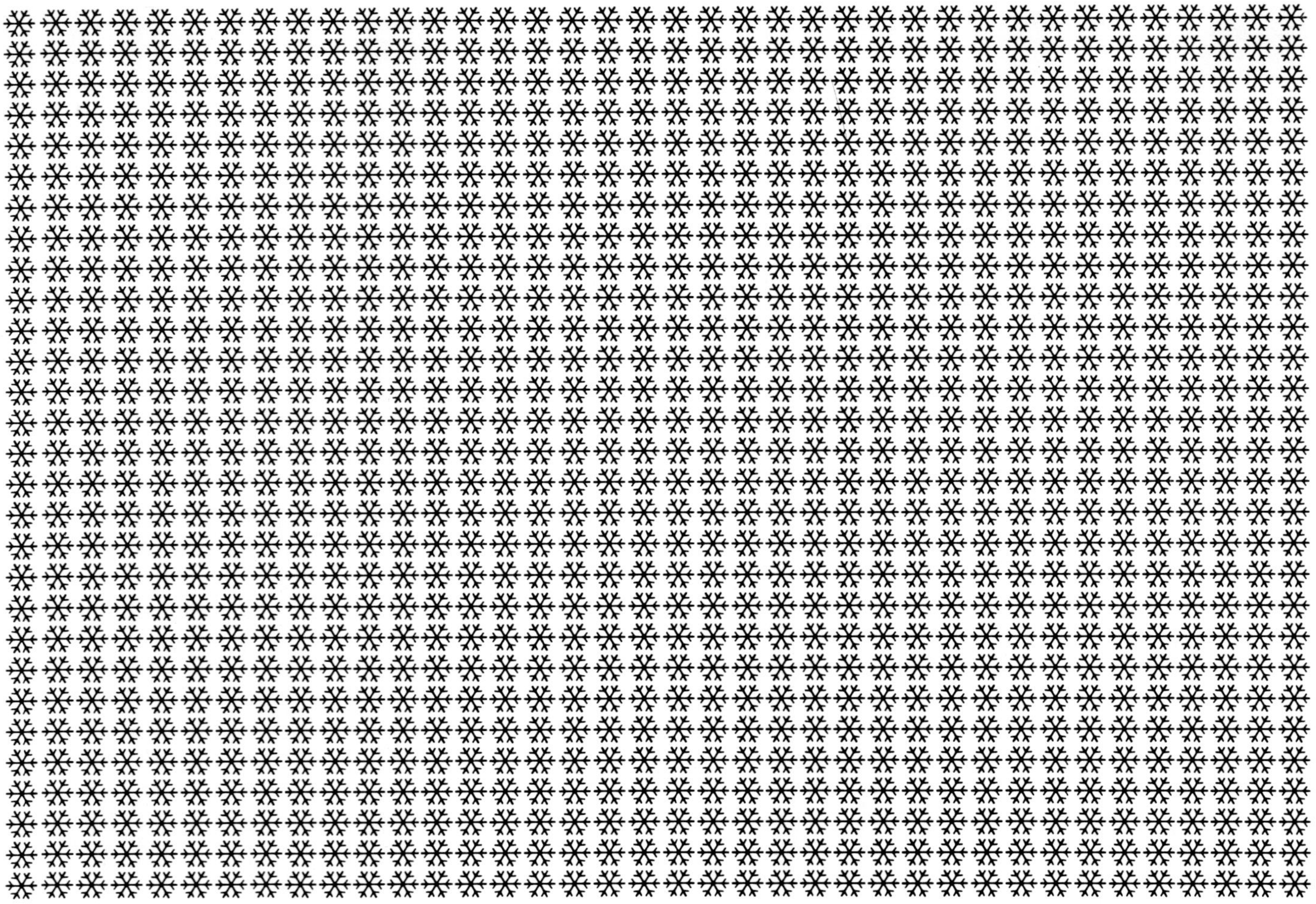

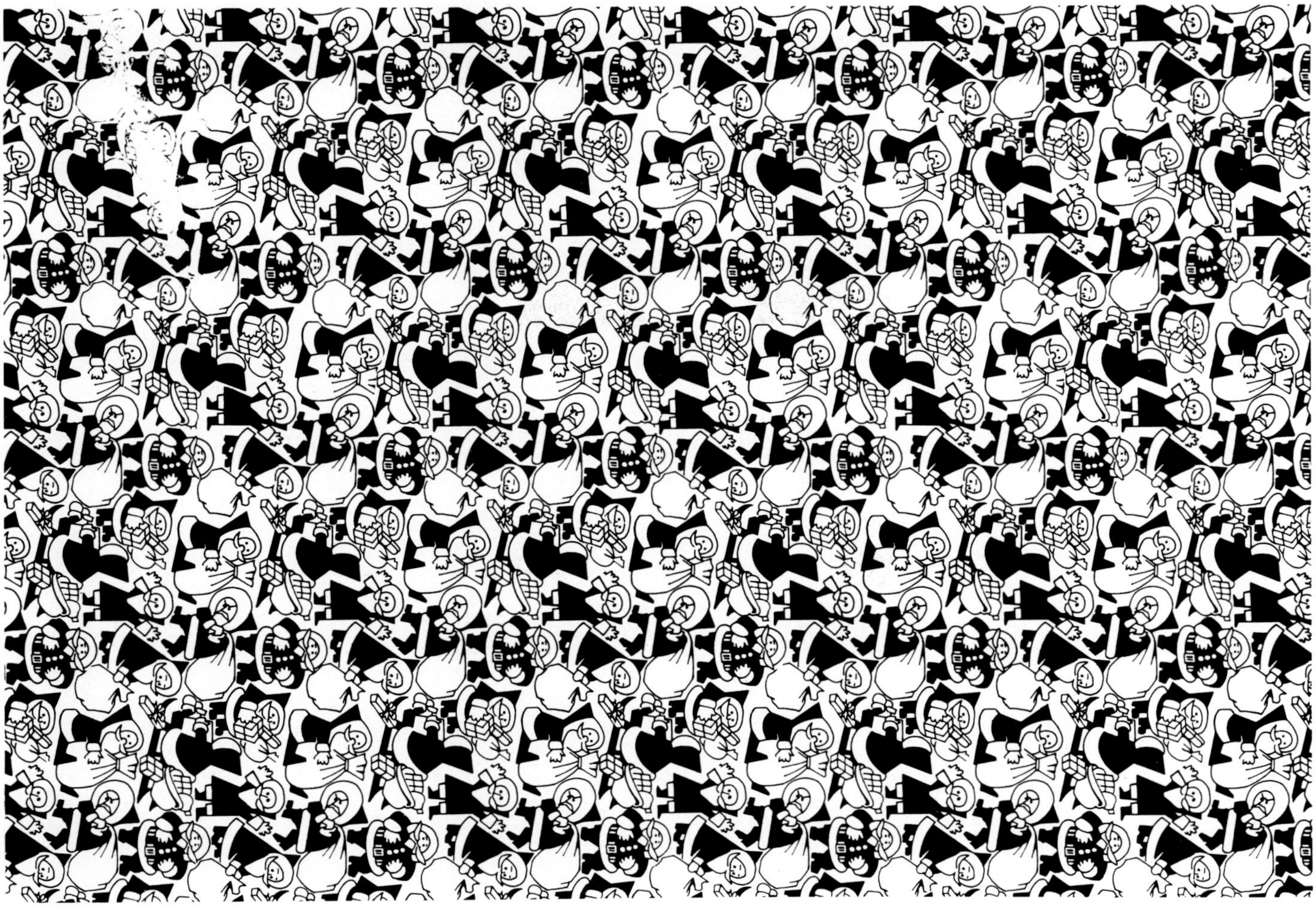

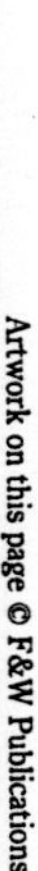

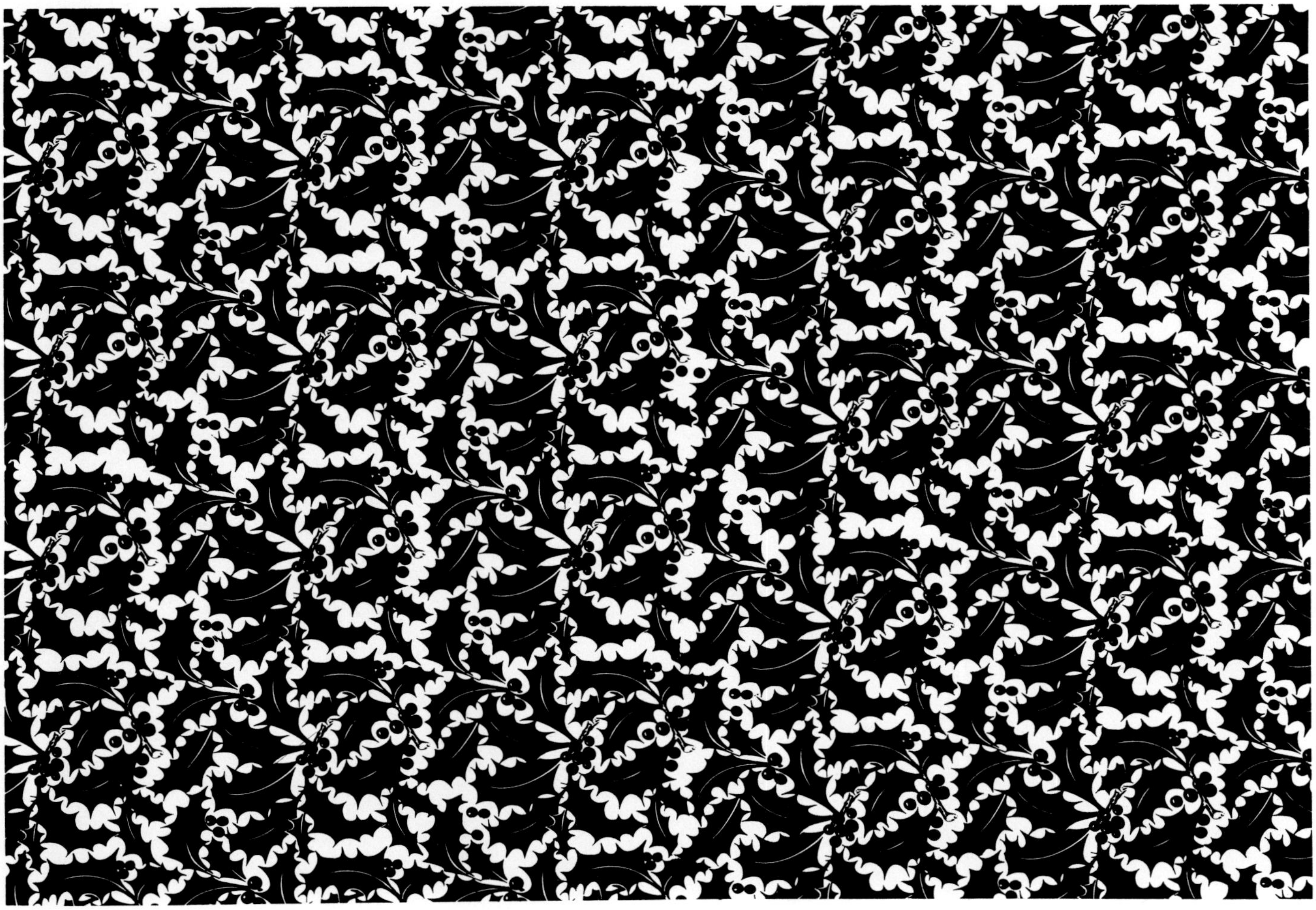

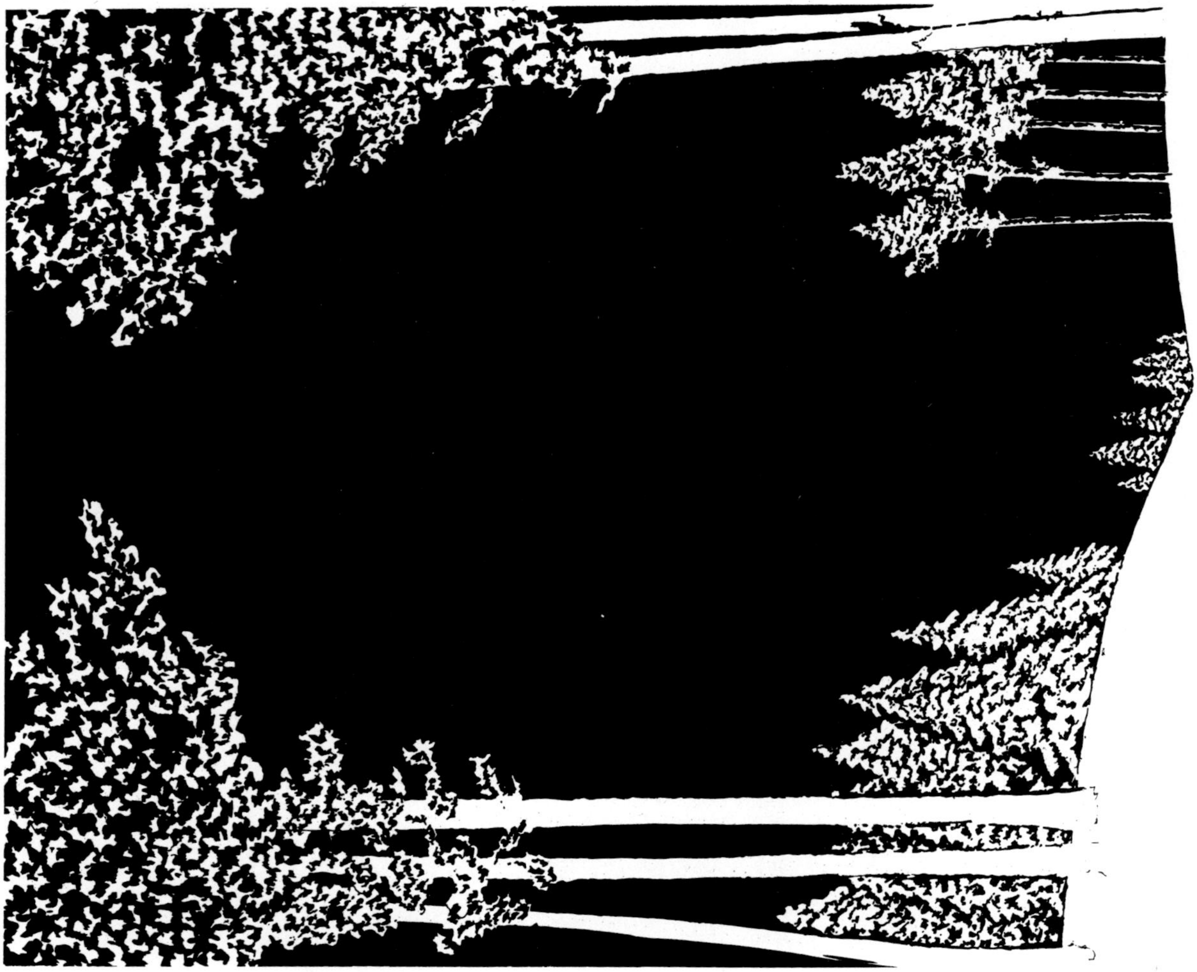

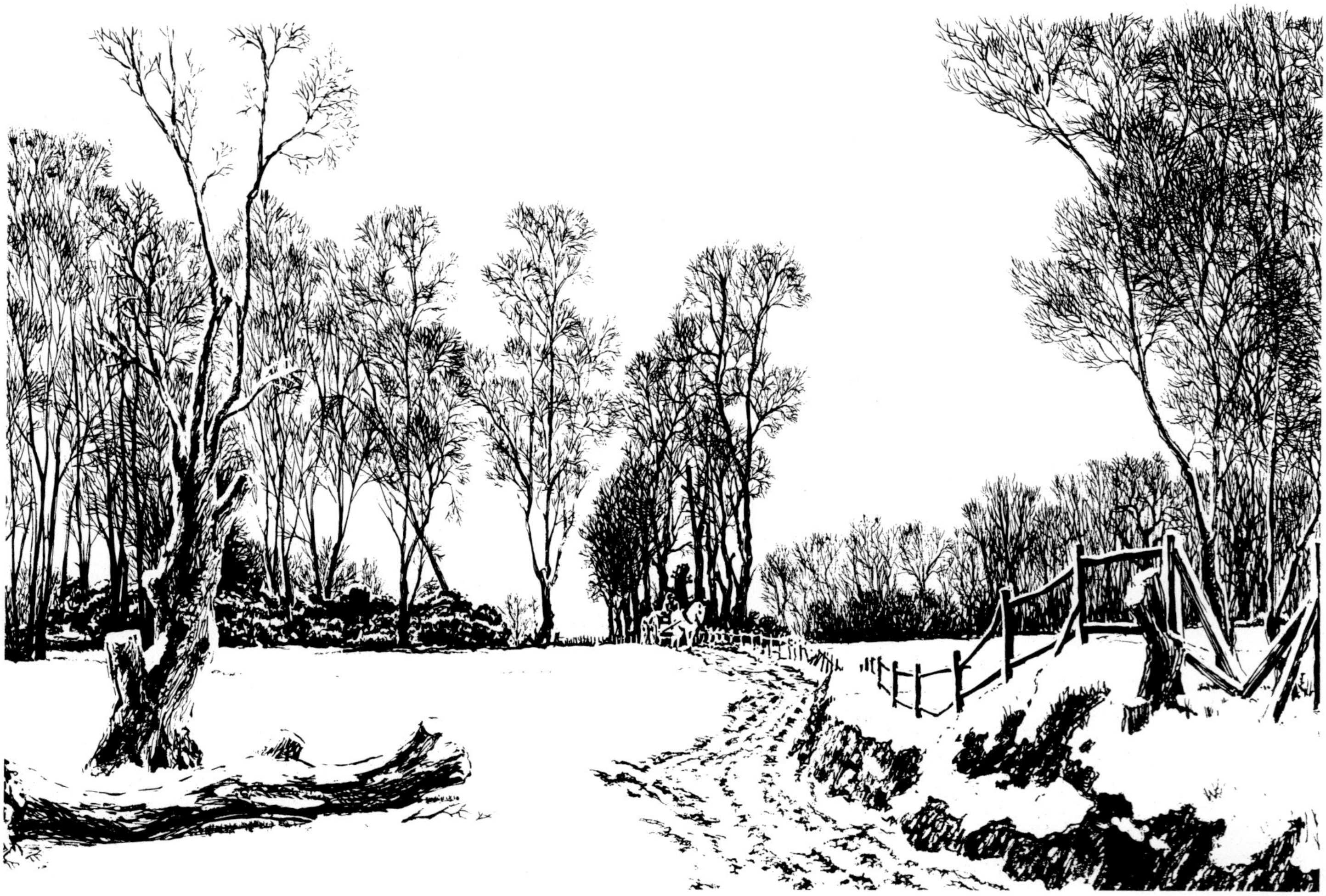

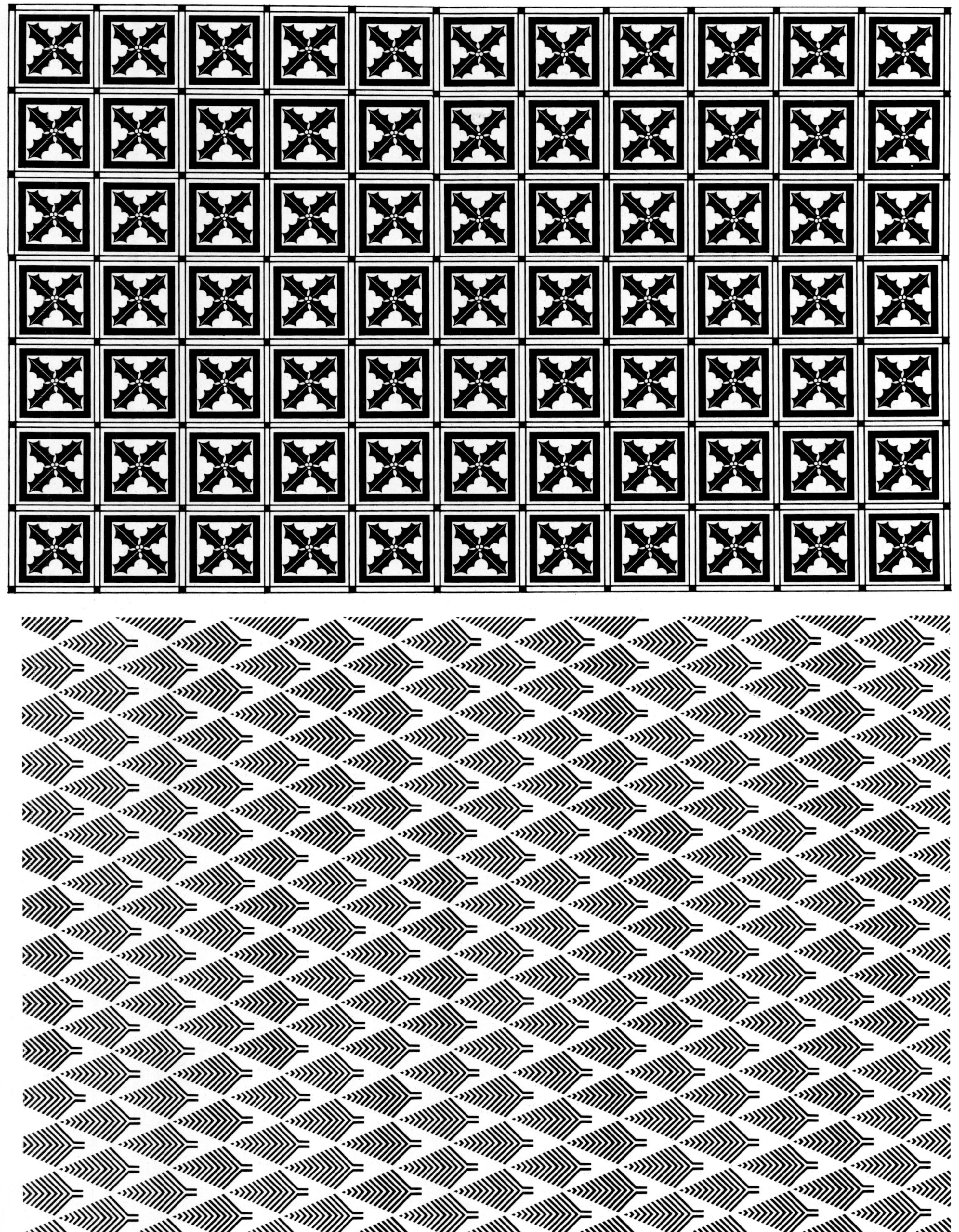

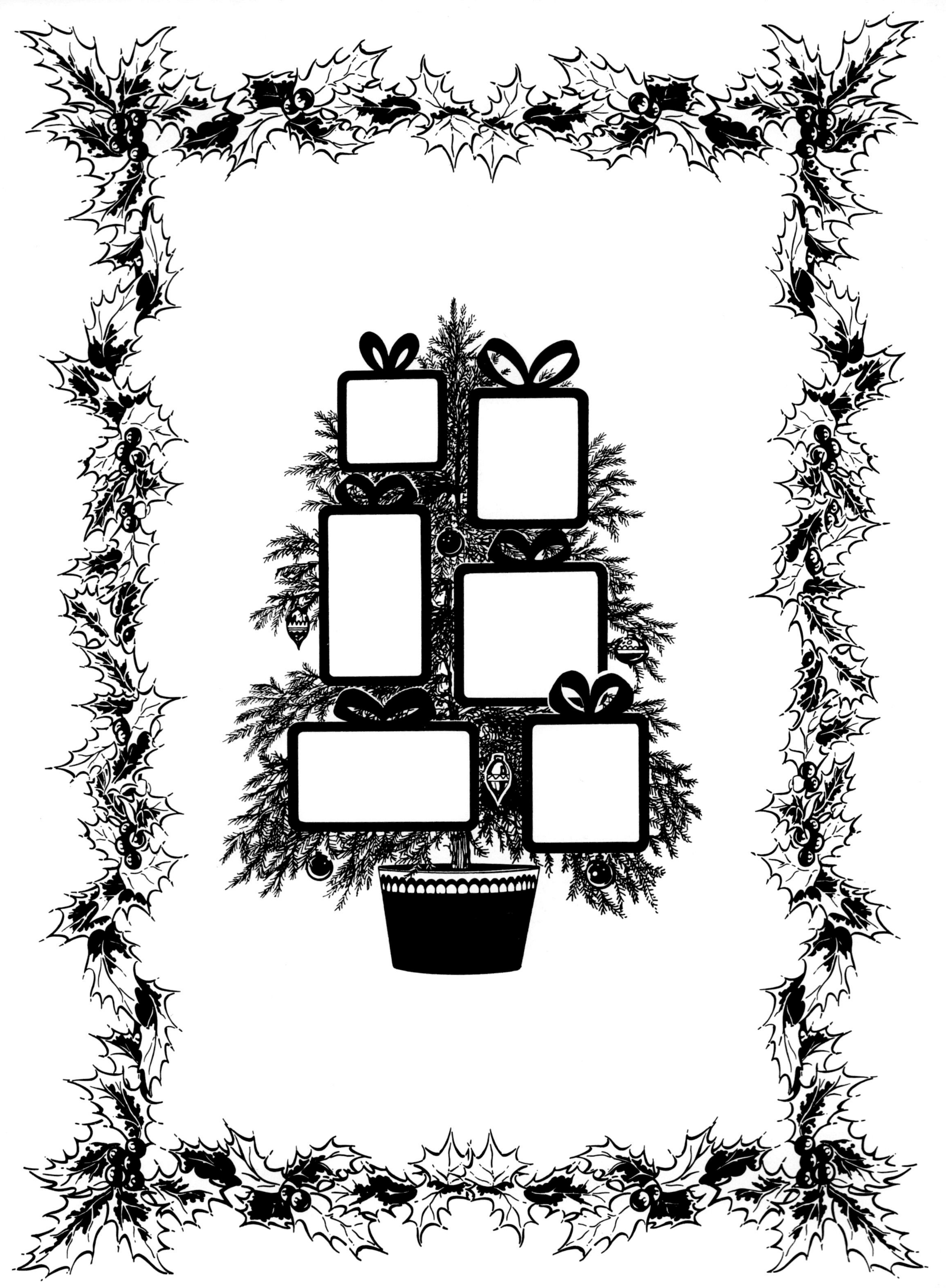

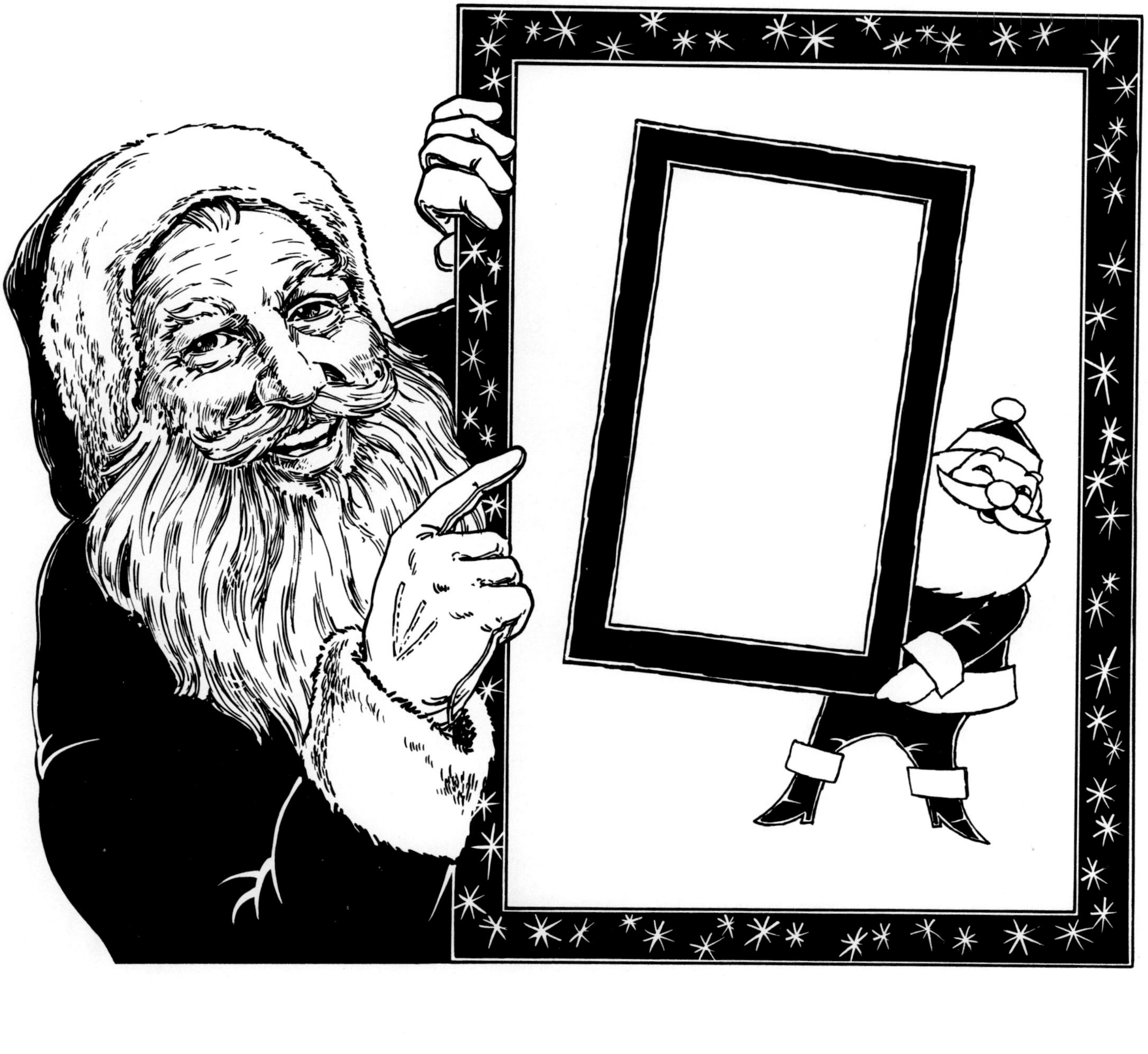

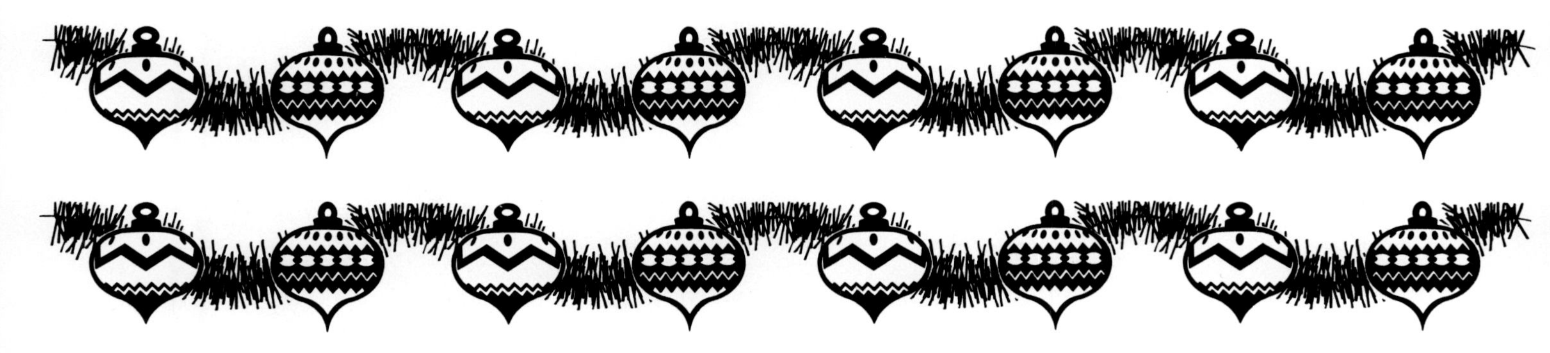

■ Borders

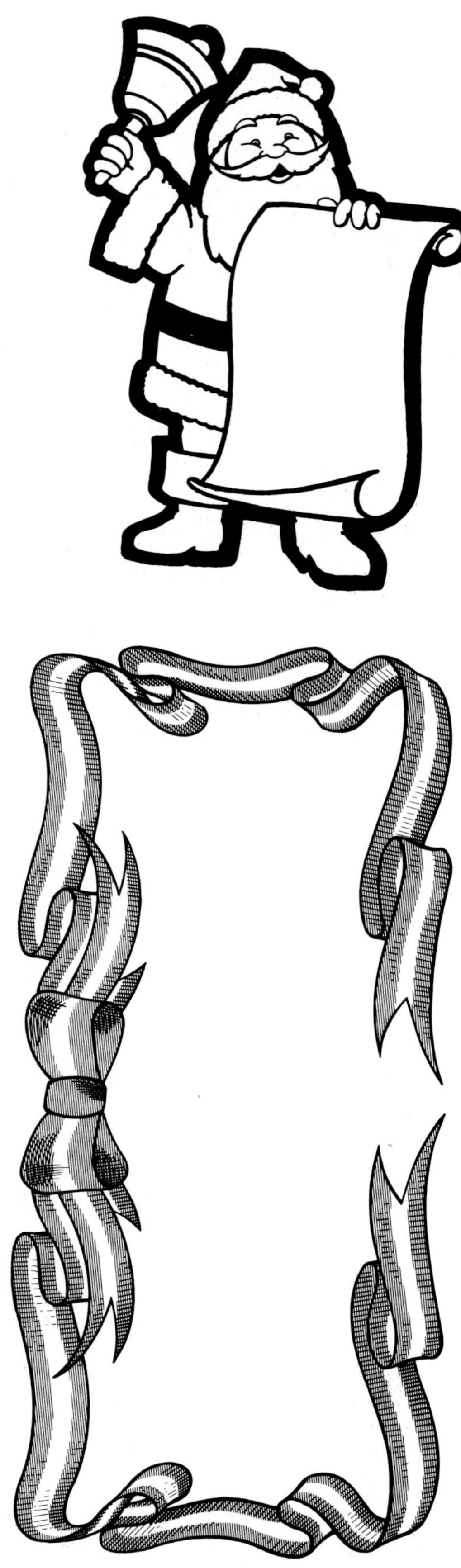

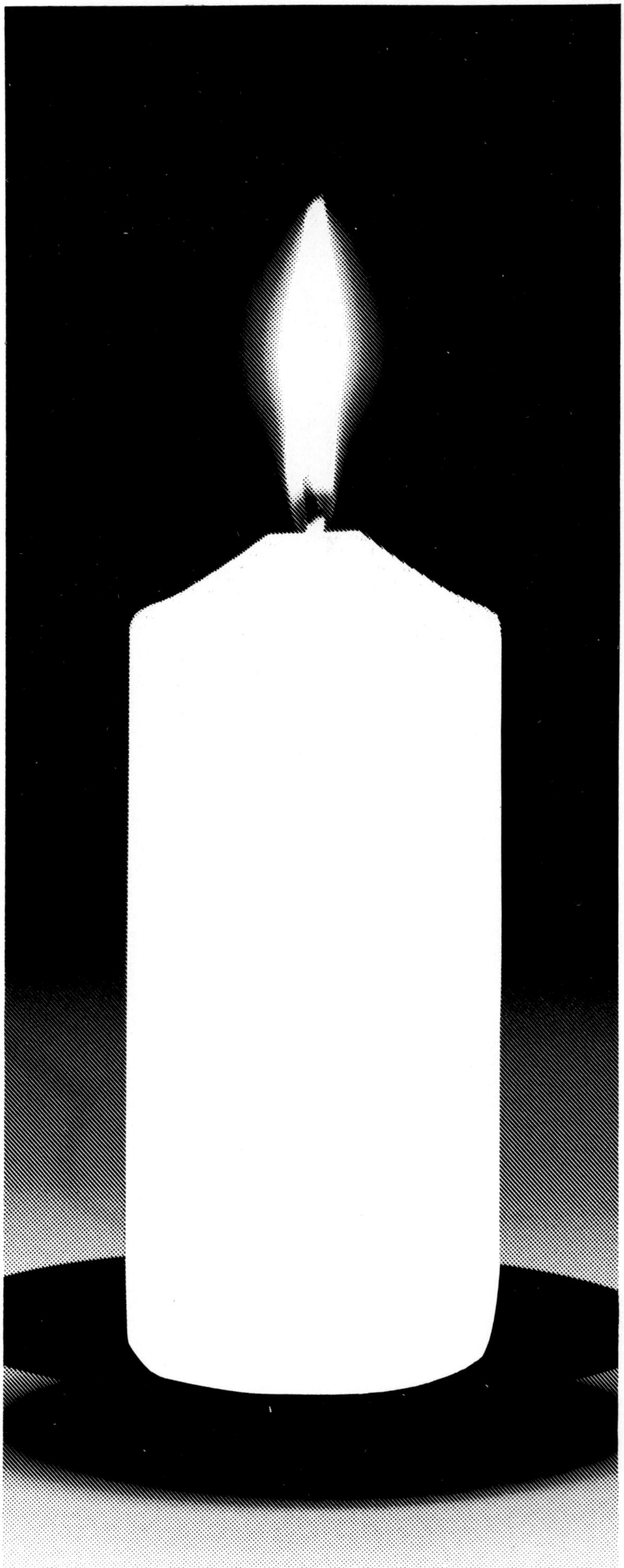

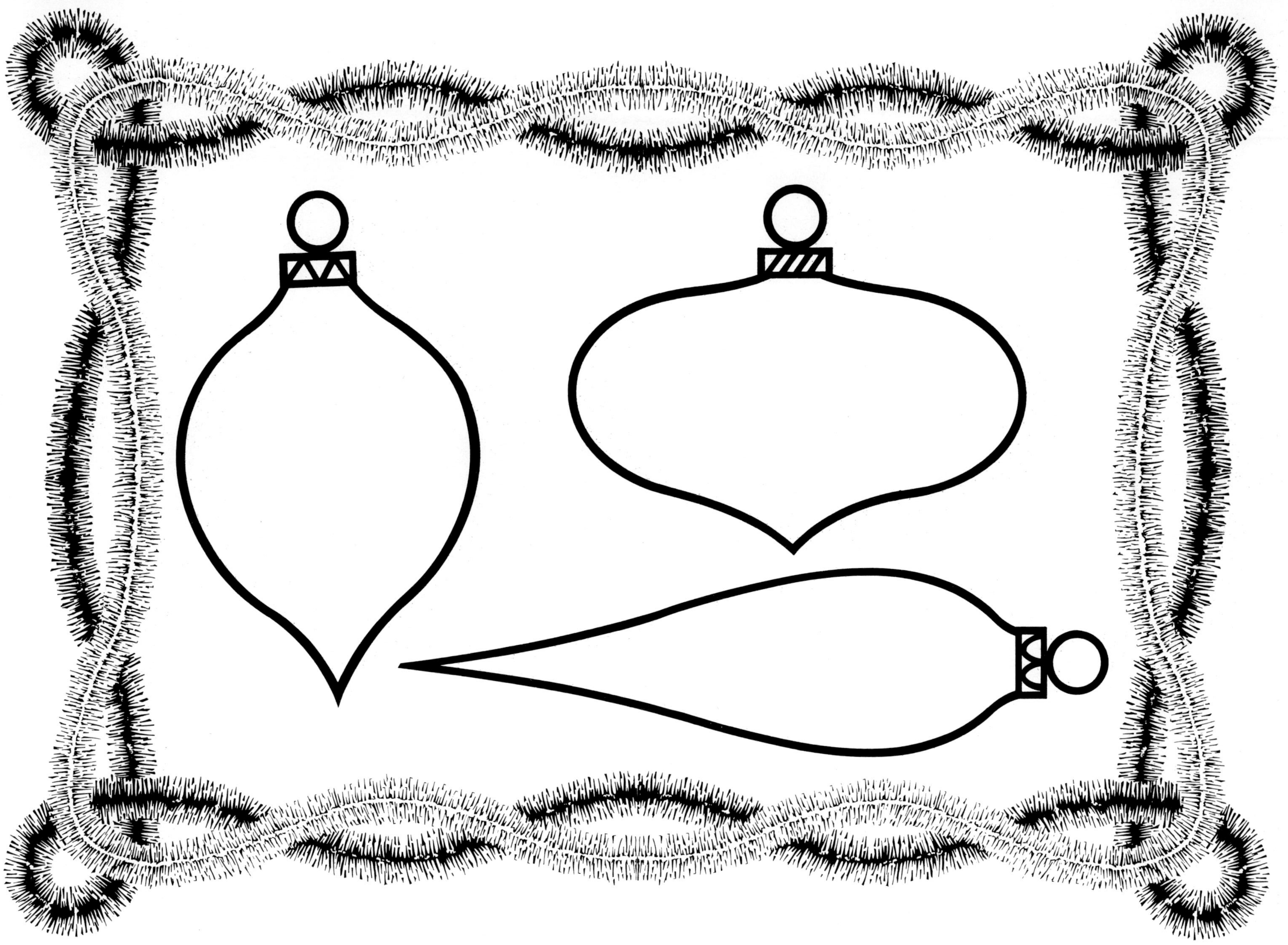

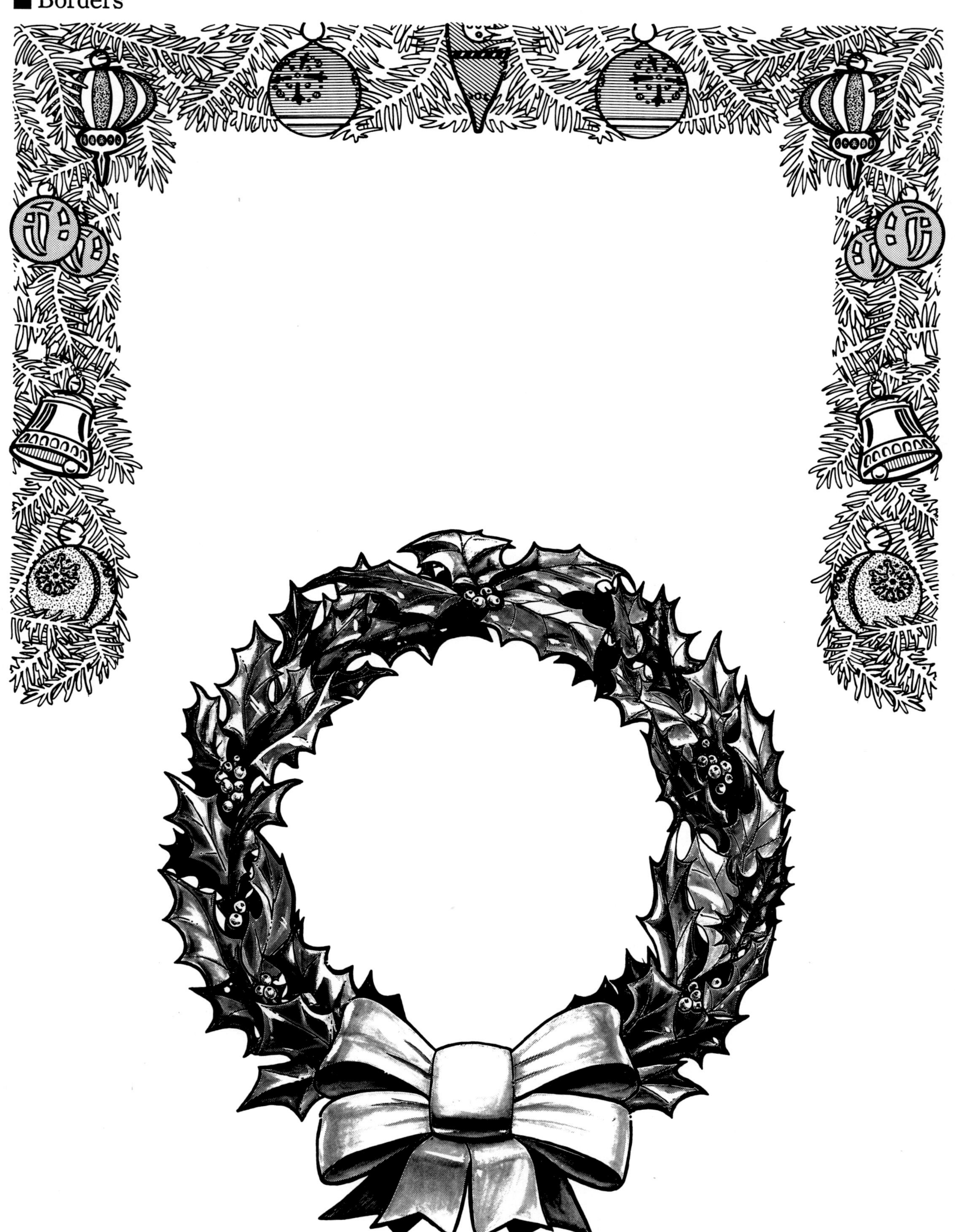

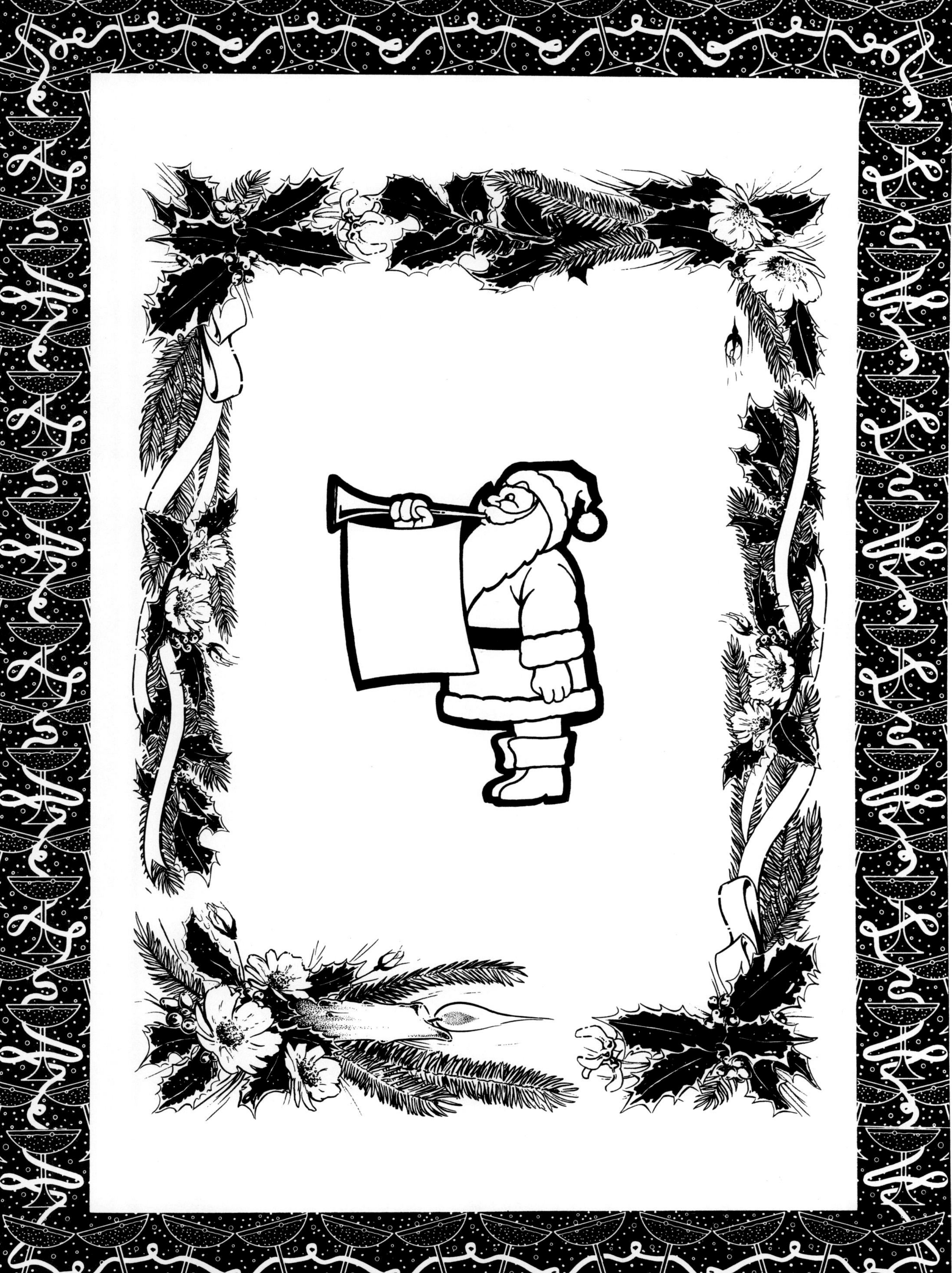

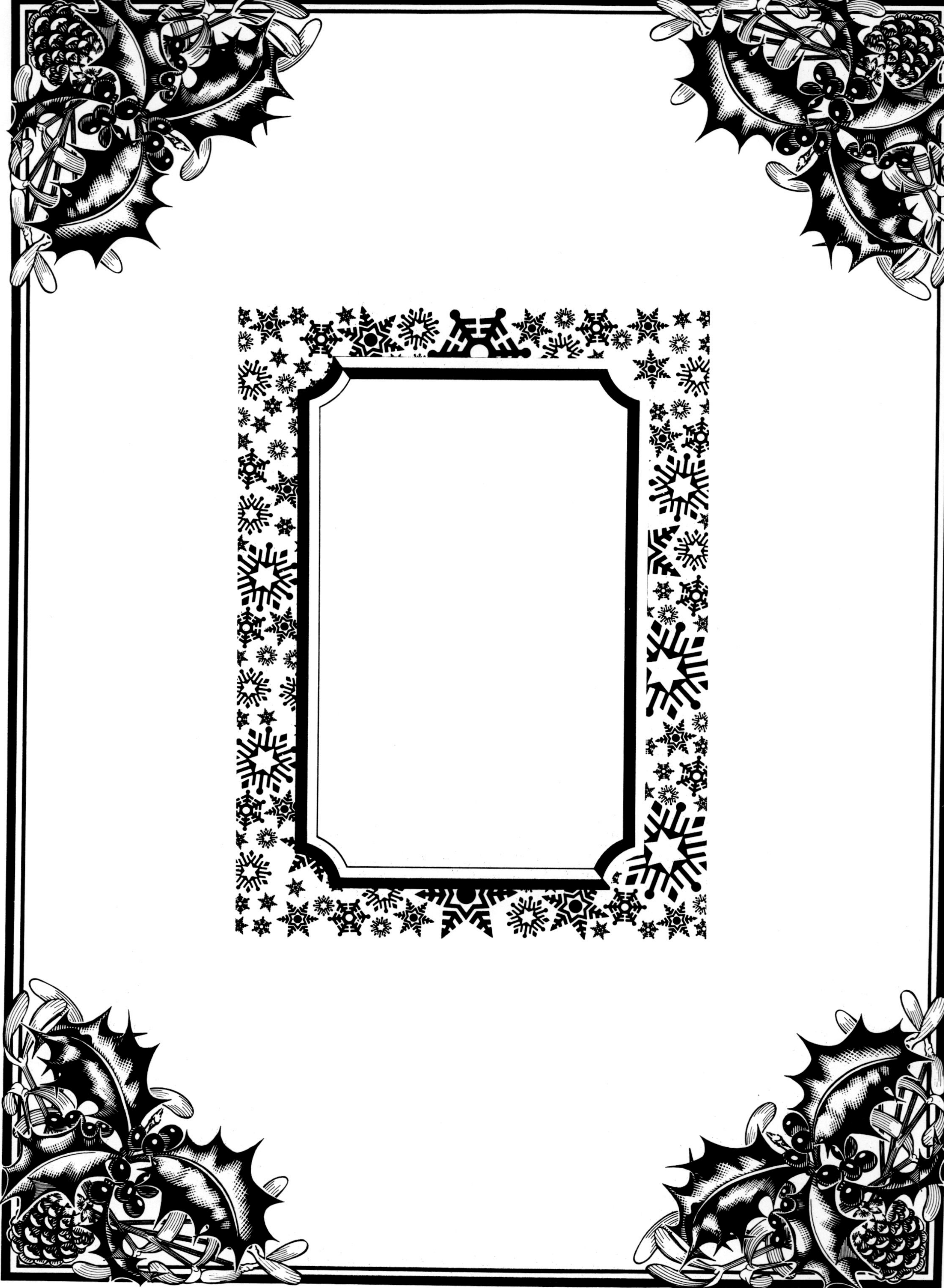

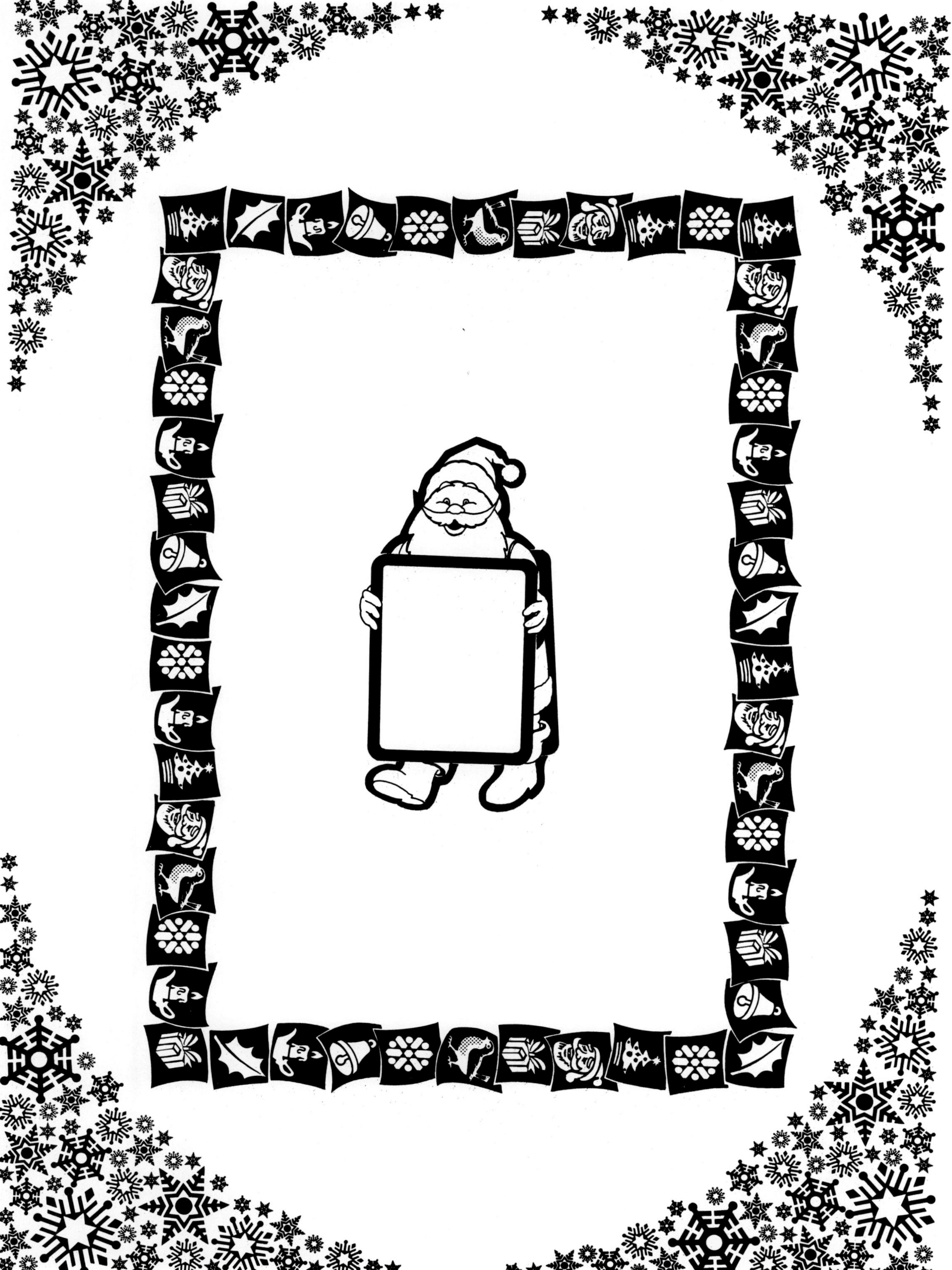

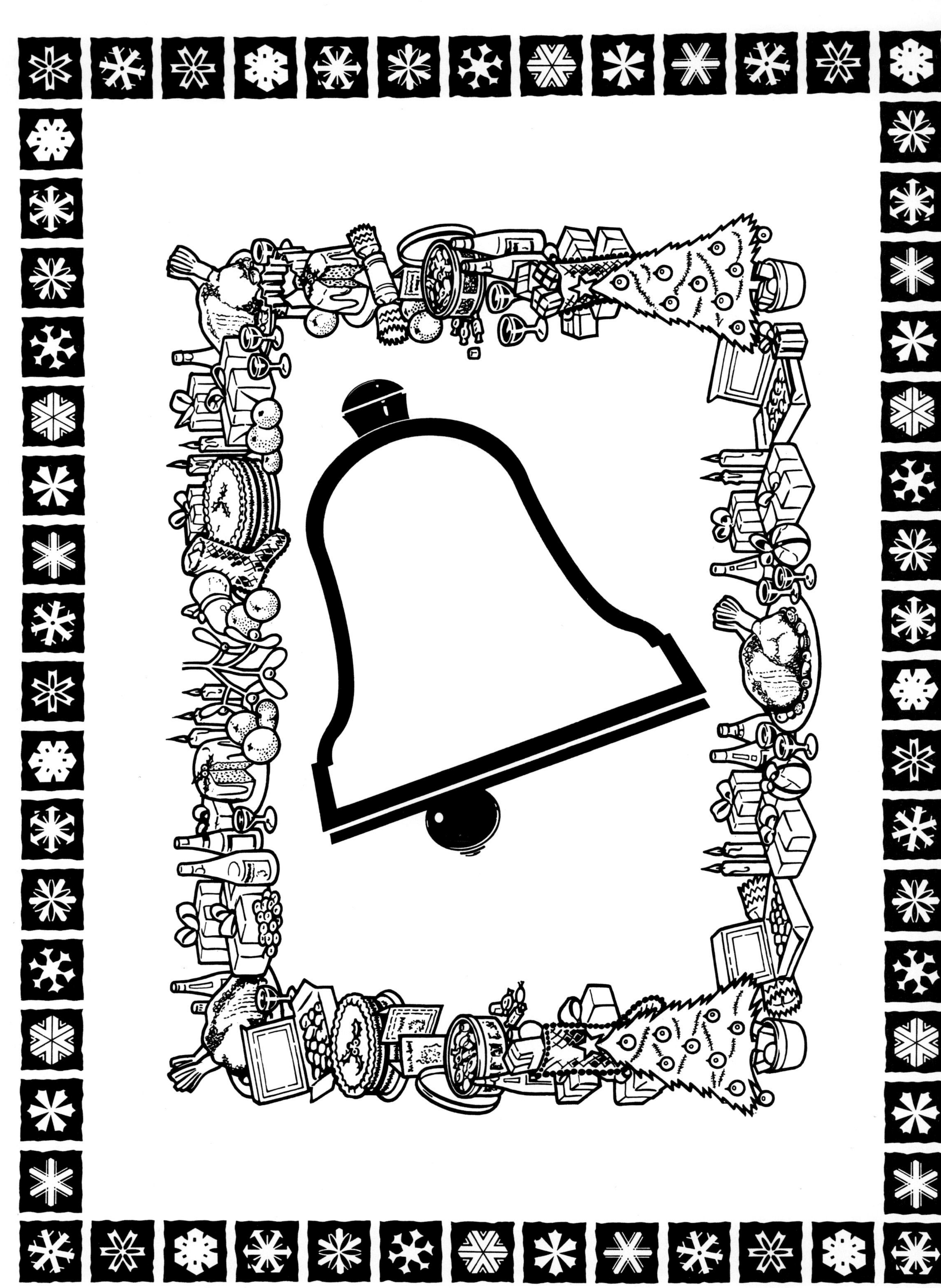

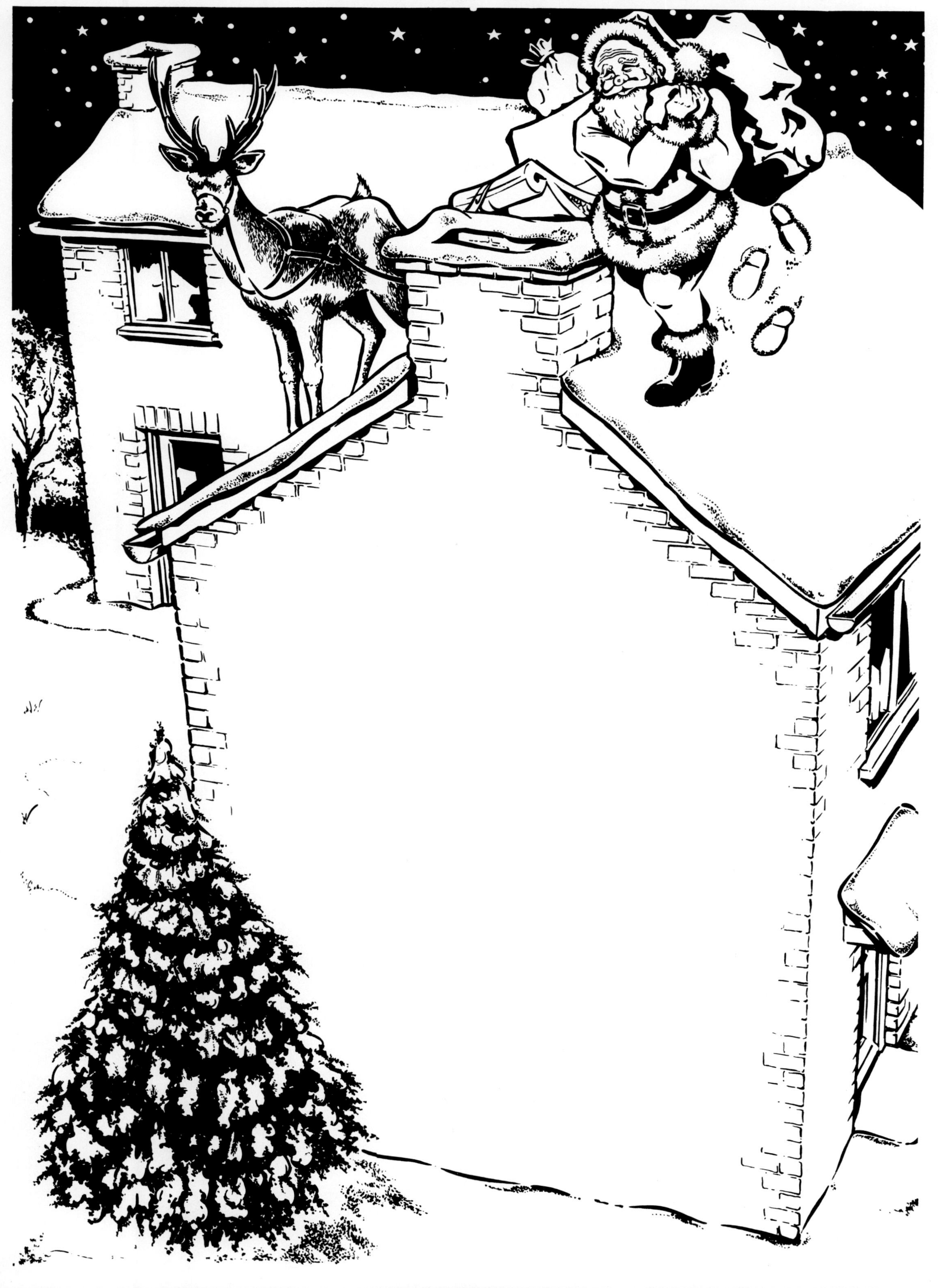

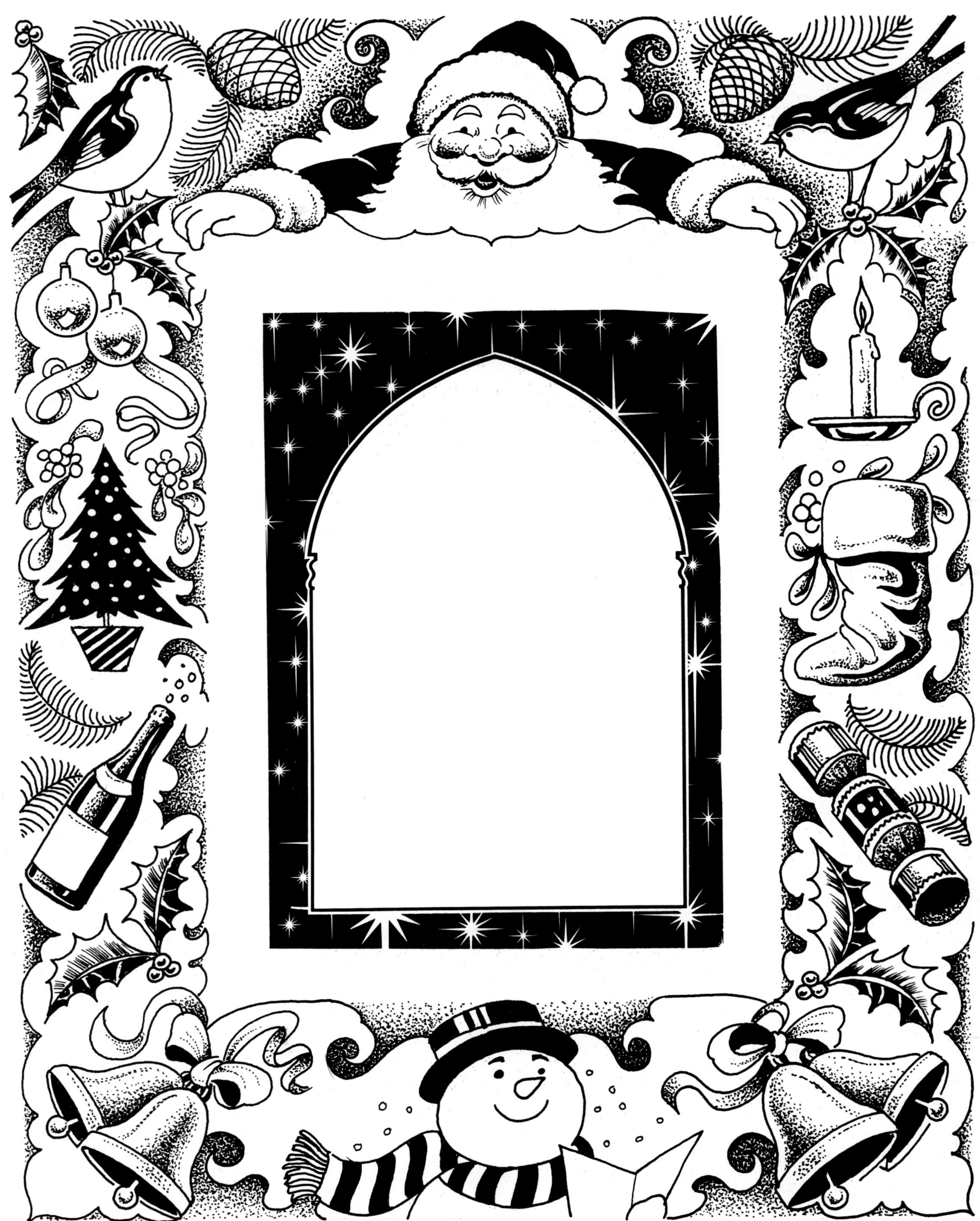